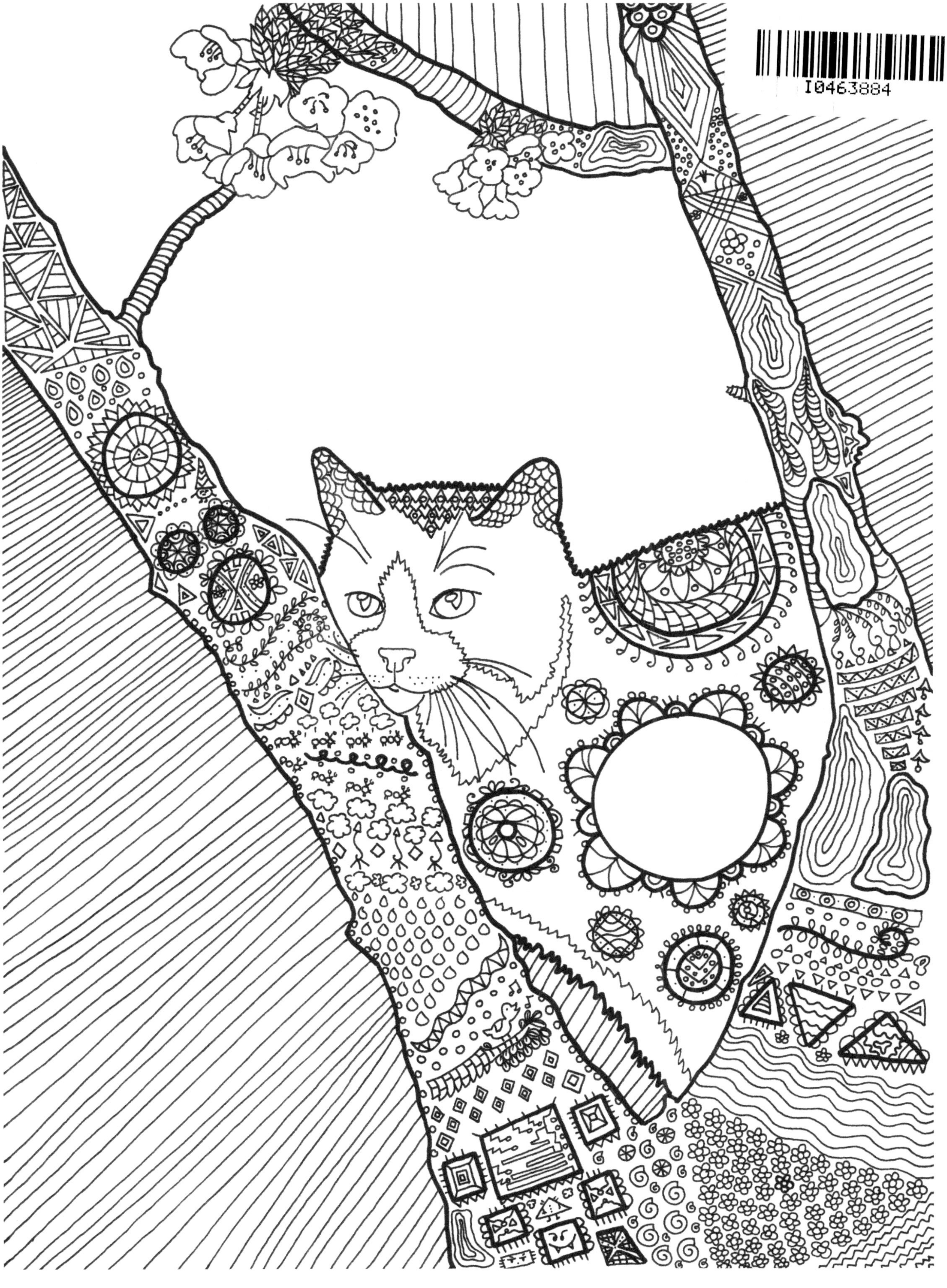

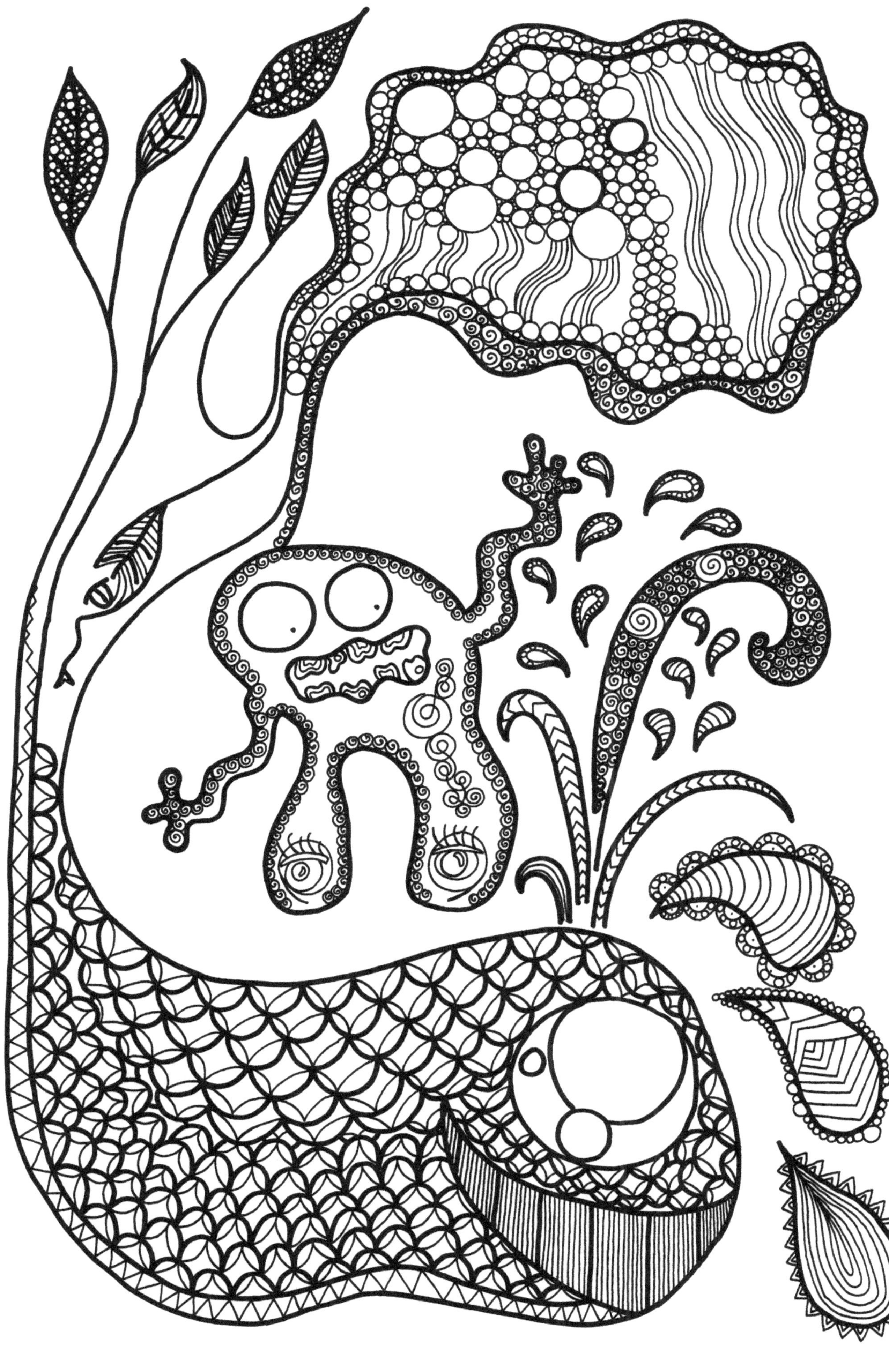

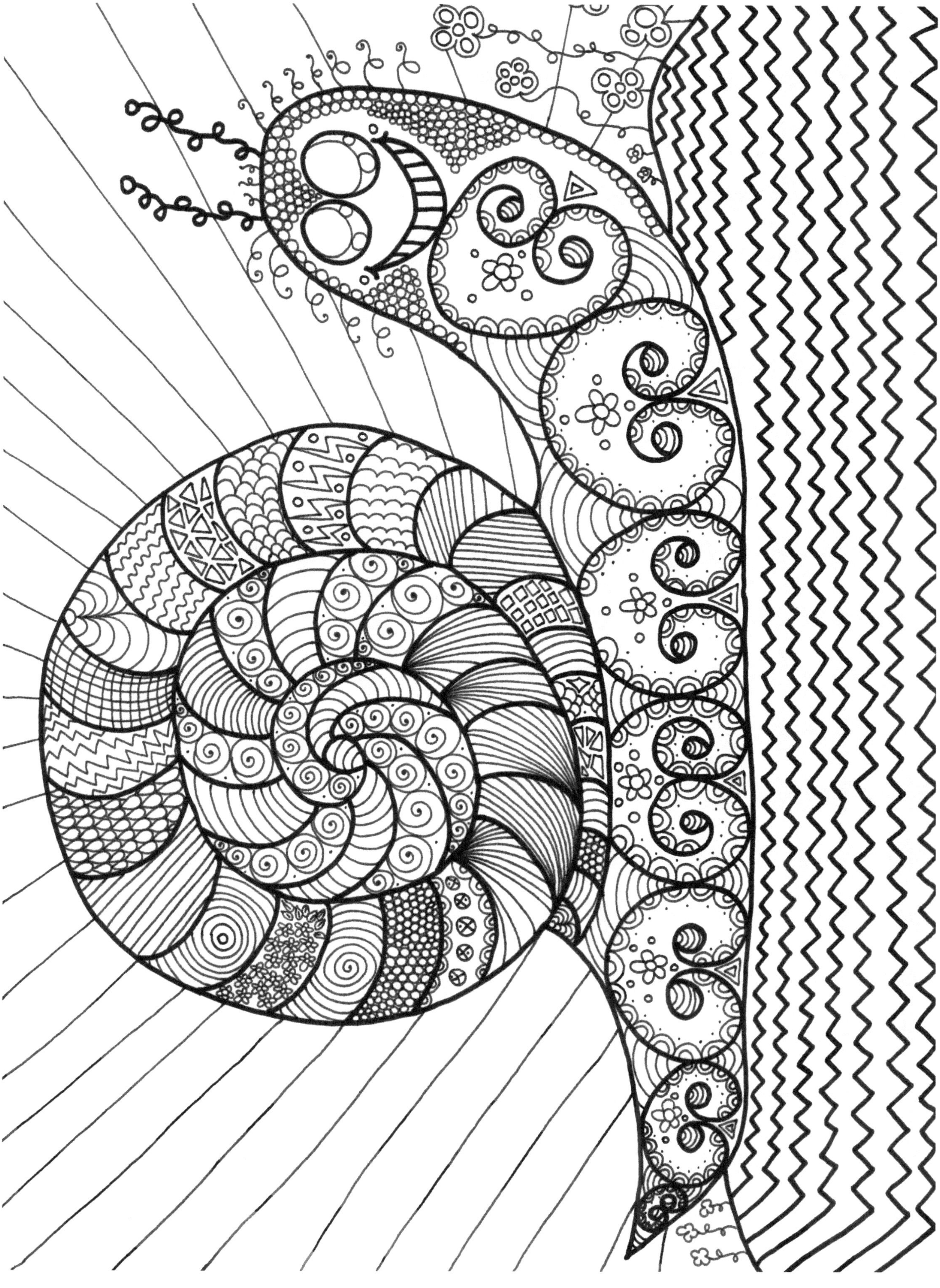

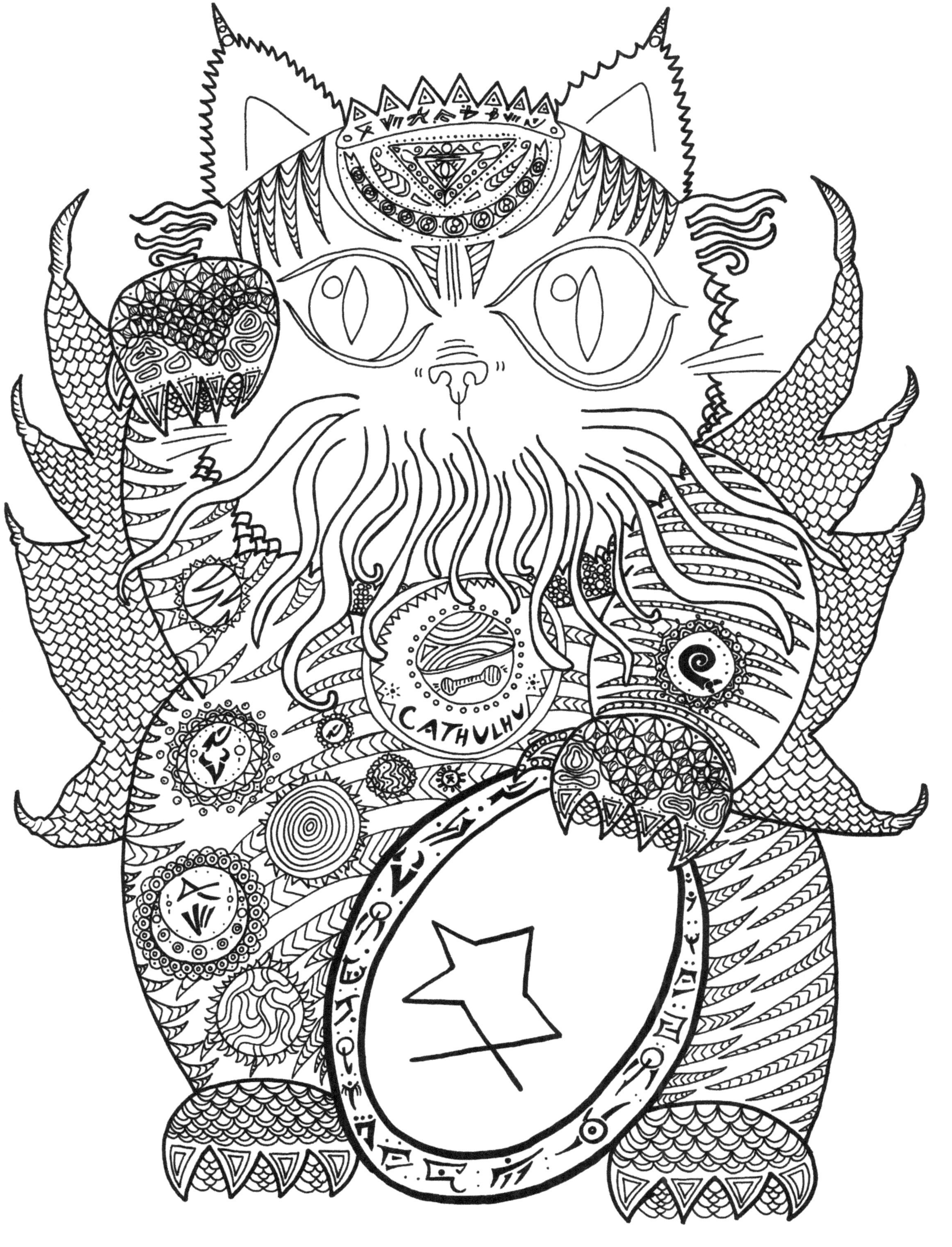
CATHULHU

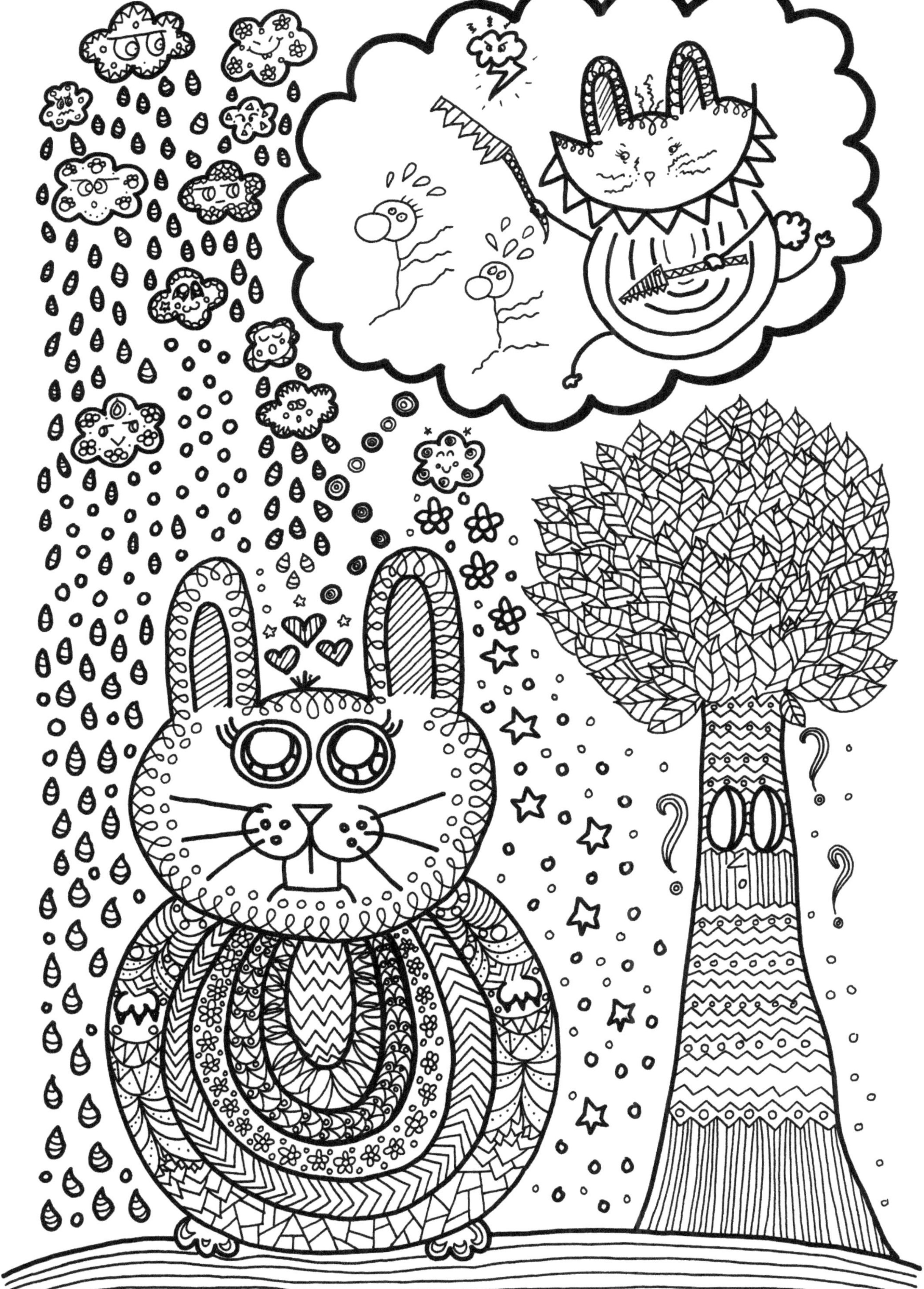

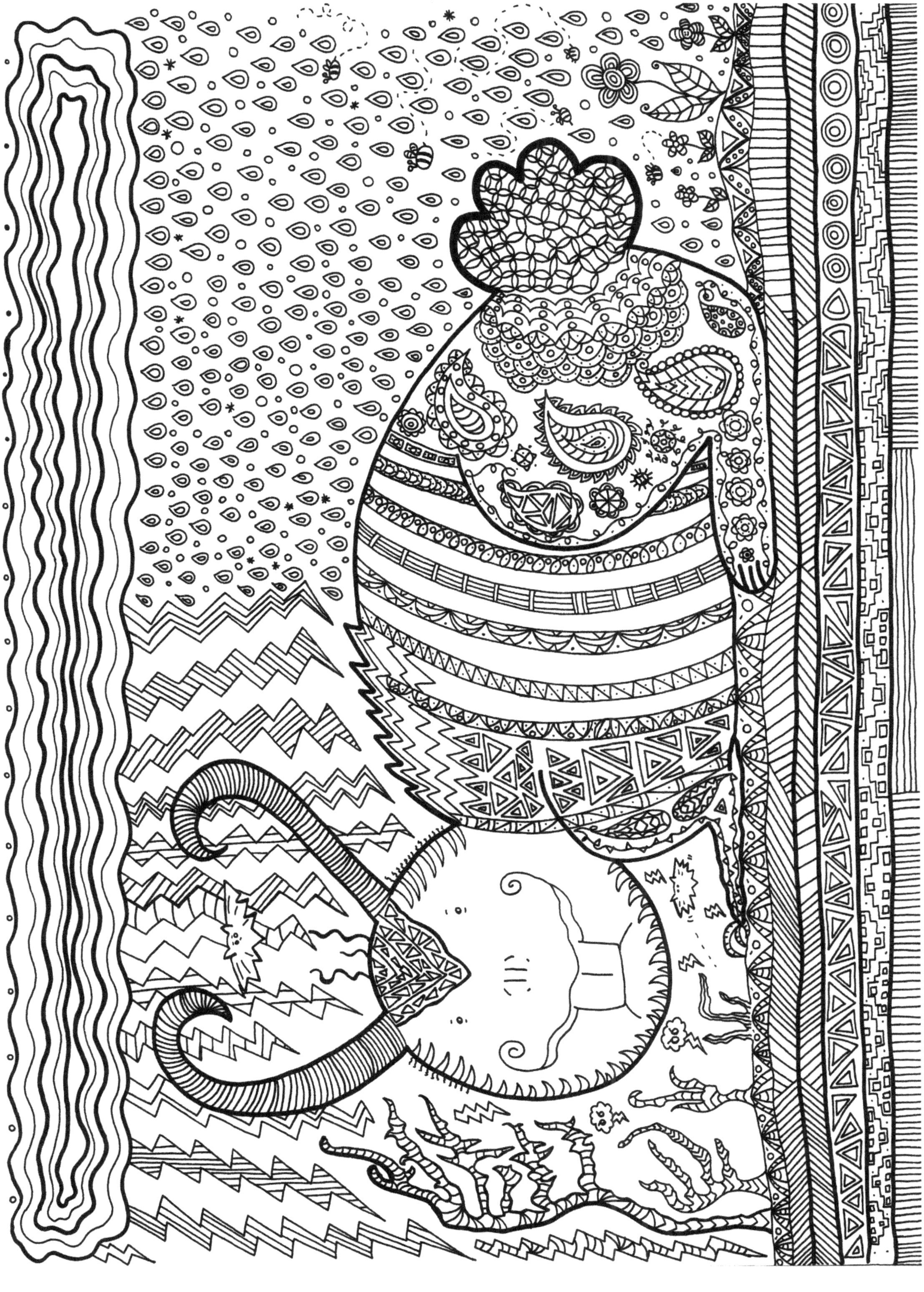

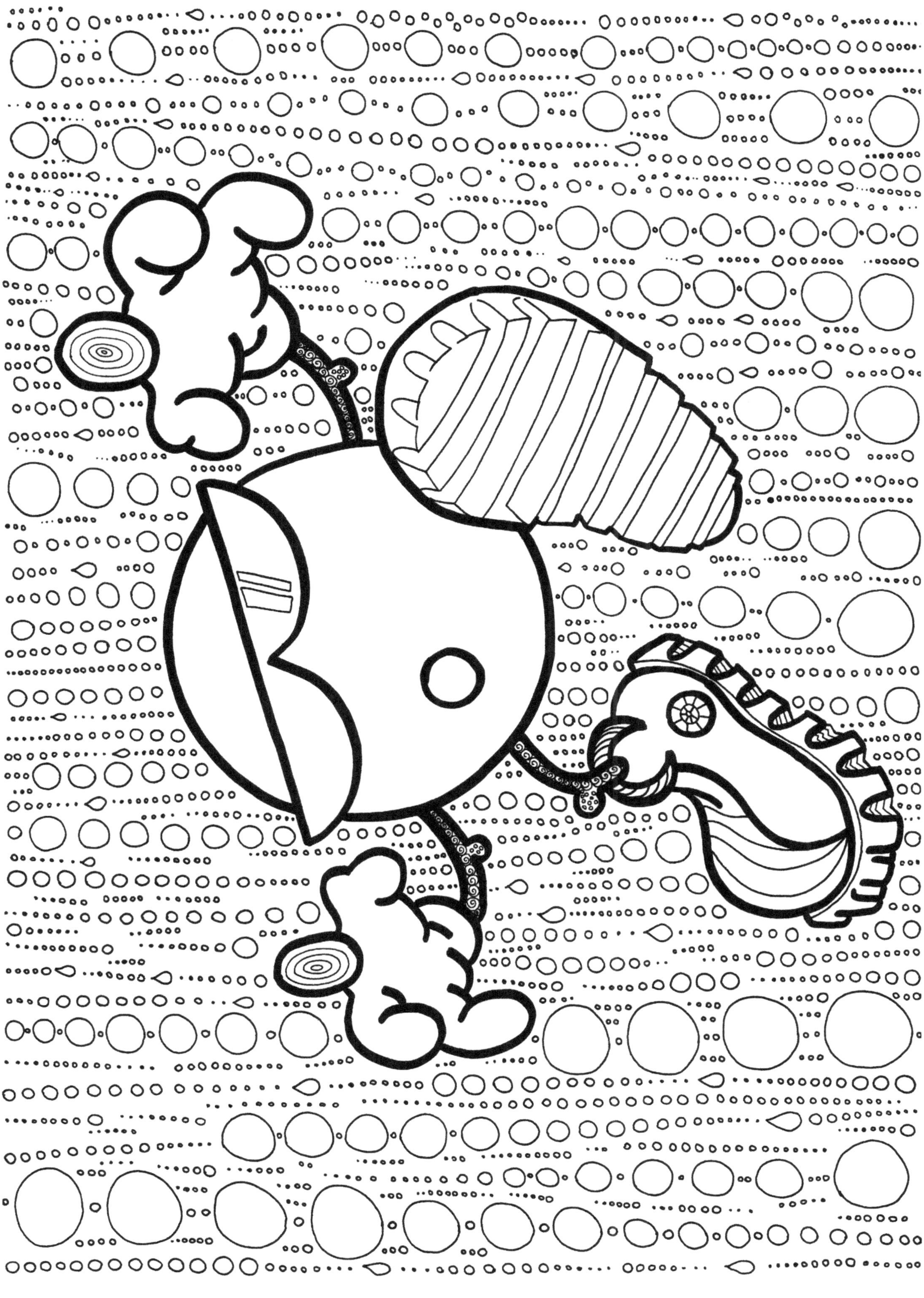

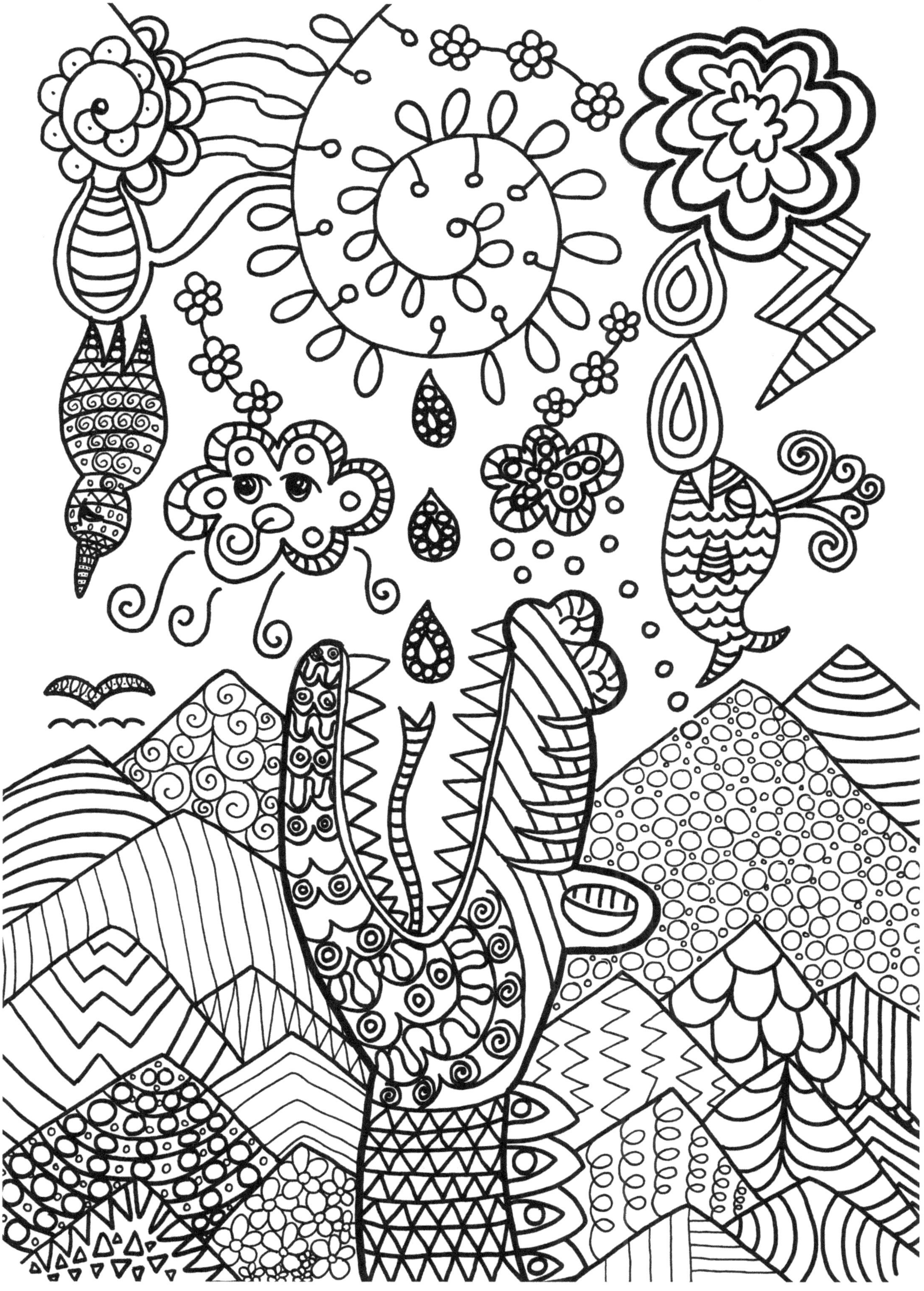

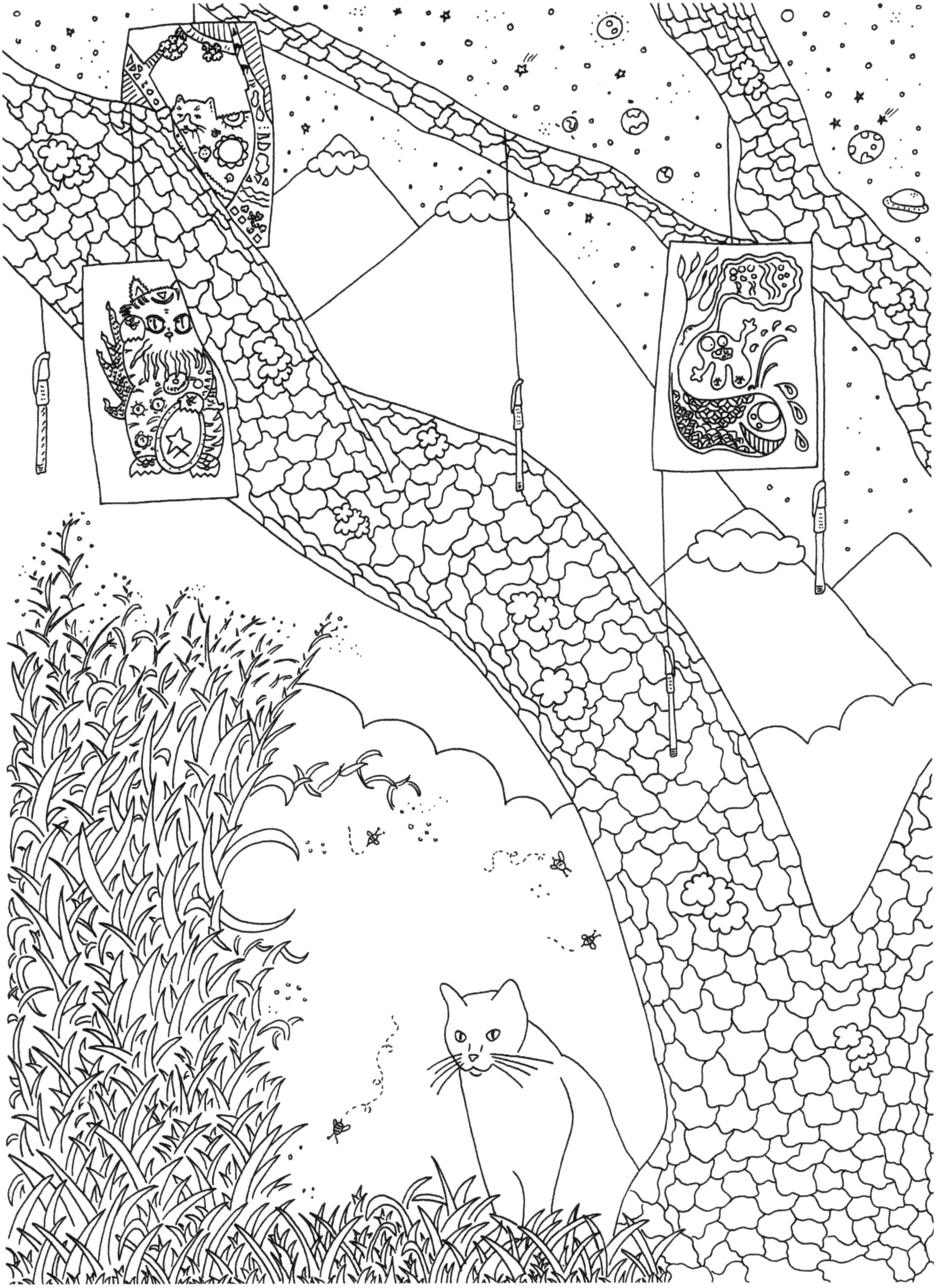

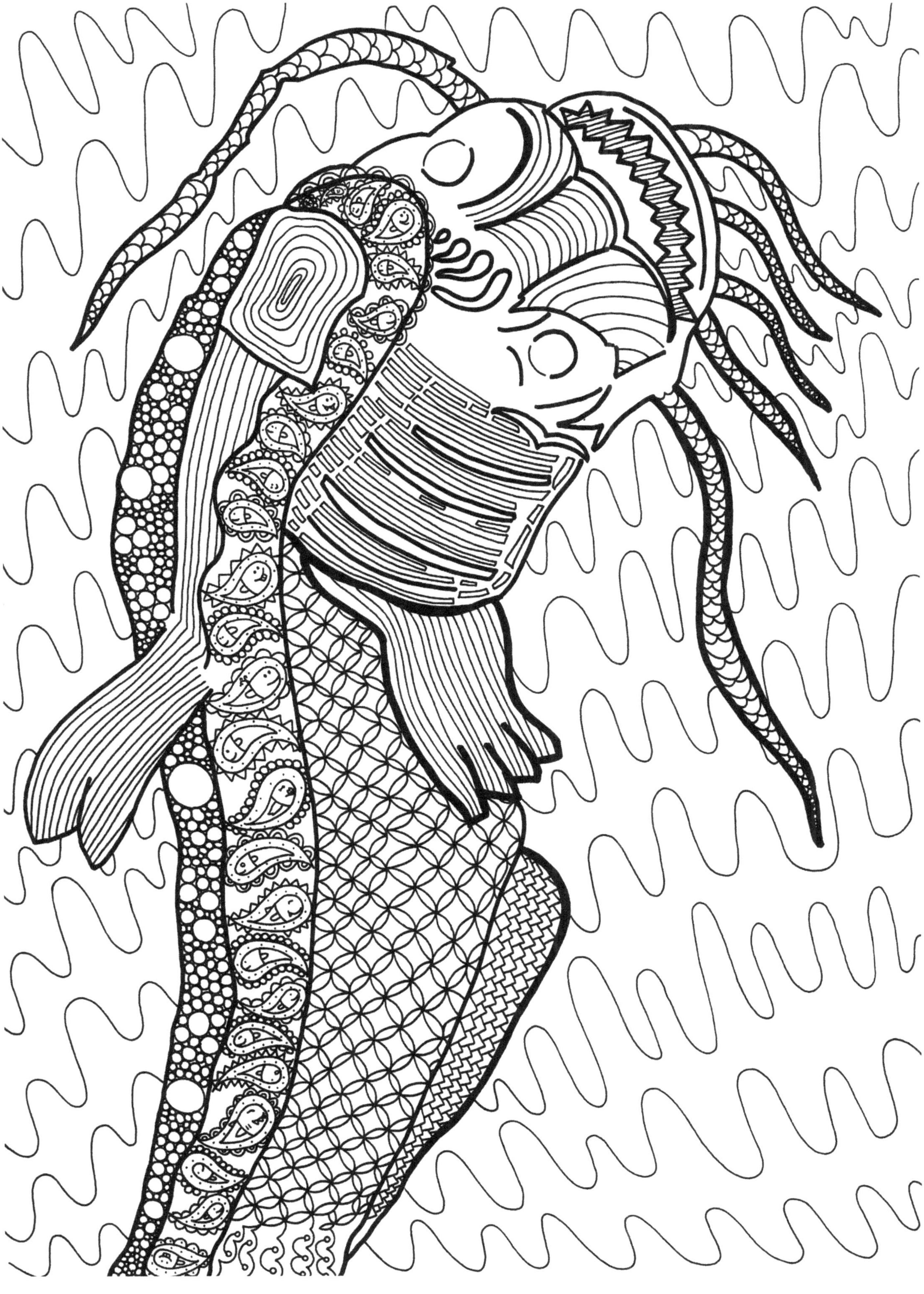

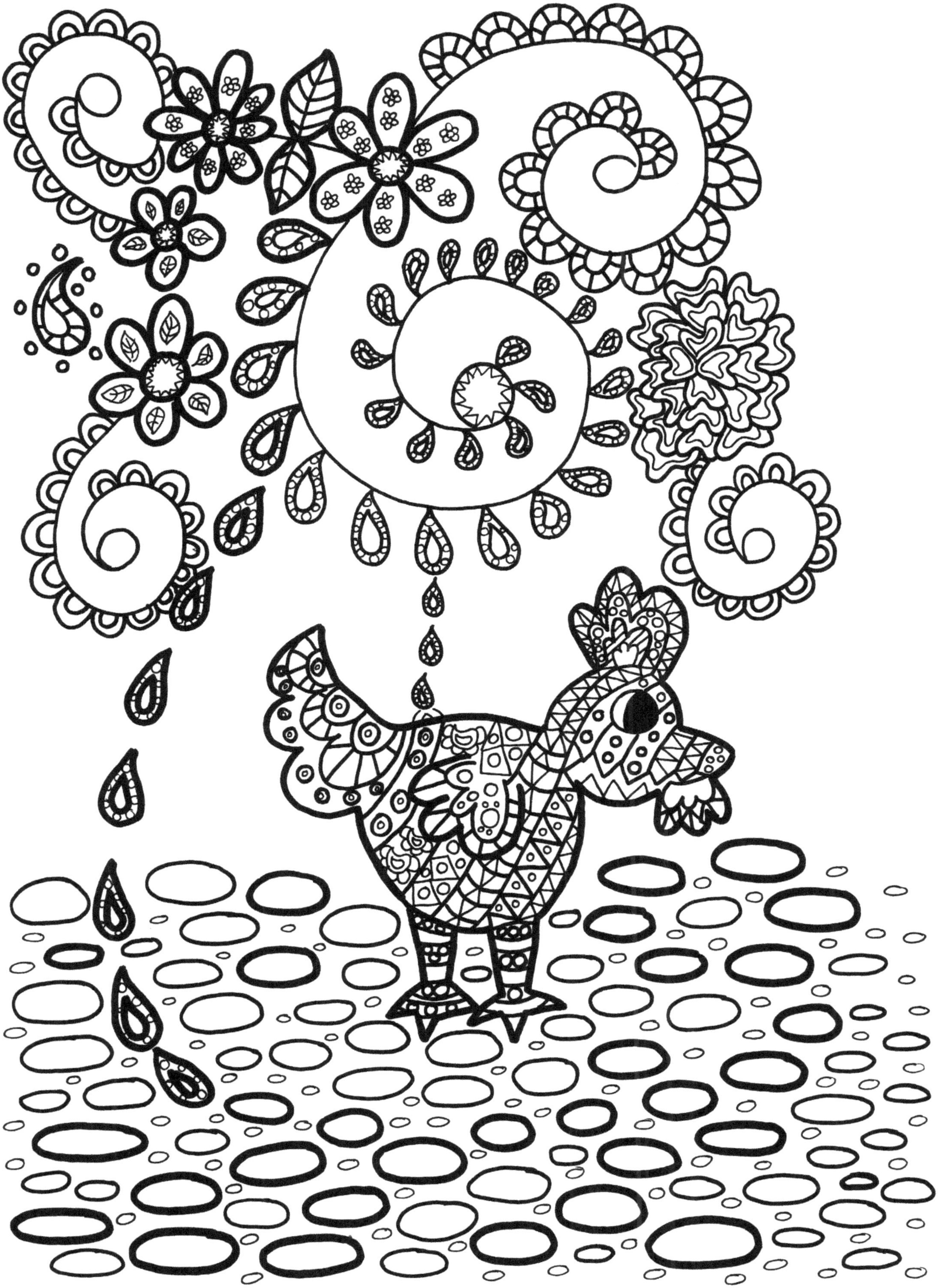

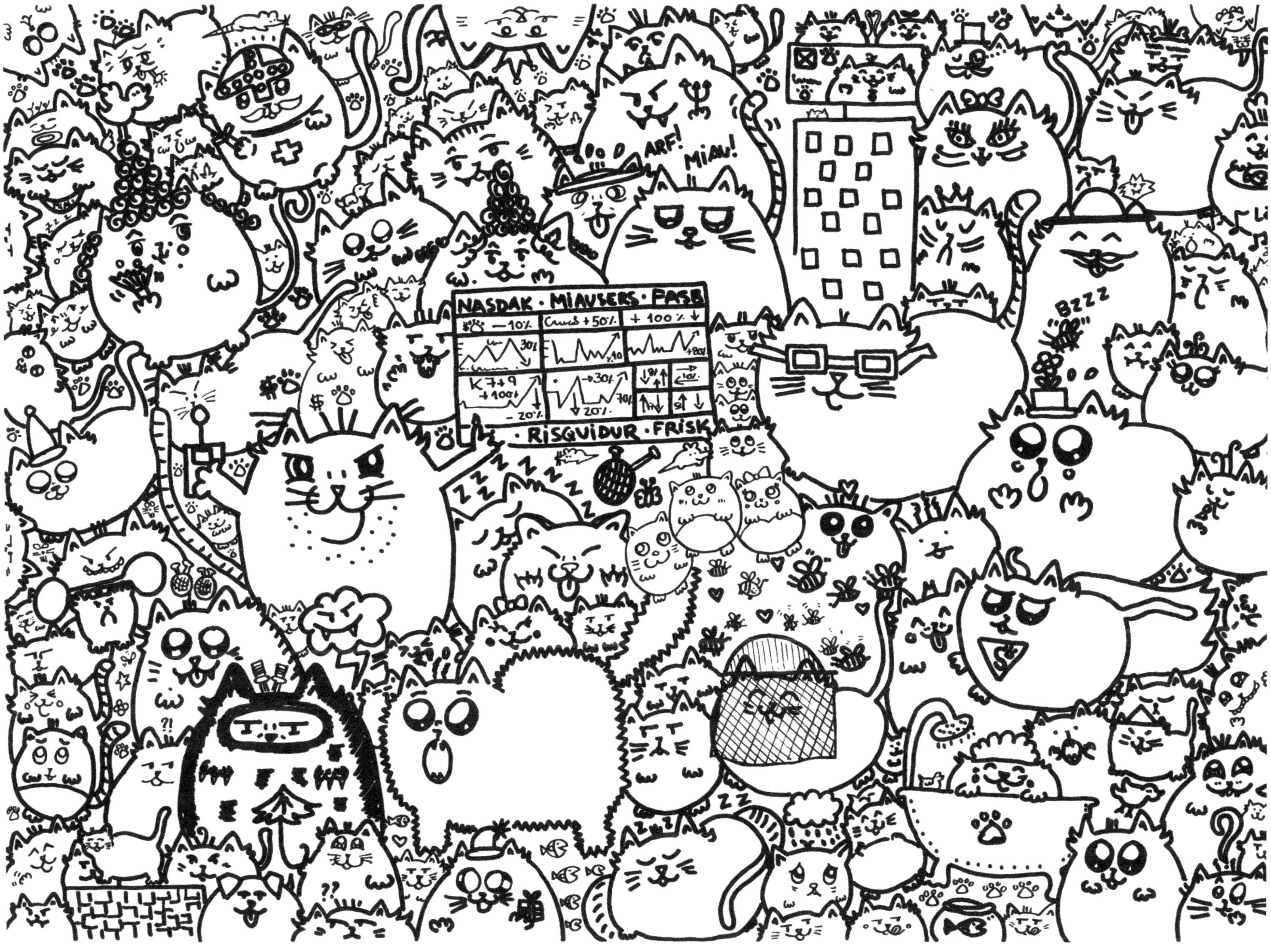

ARF!
MIAU!
NASDAK · MIAUSERS · PASB
· RISQUIDUR · FRISK

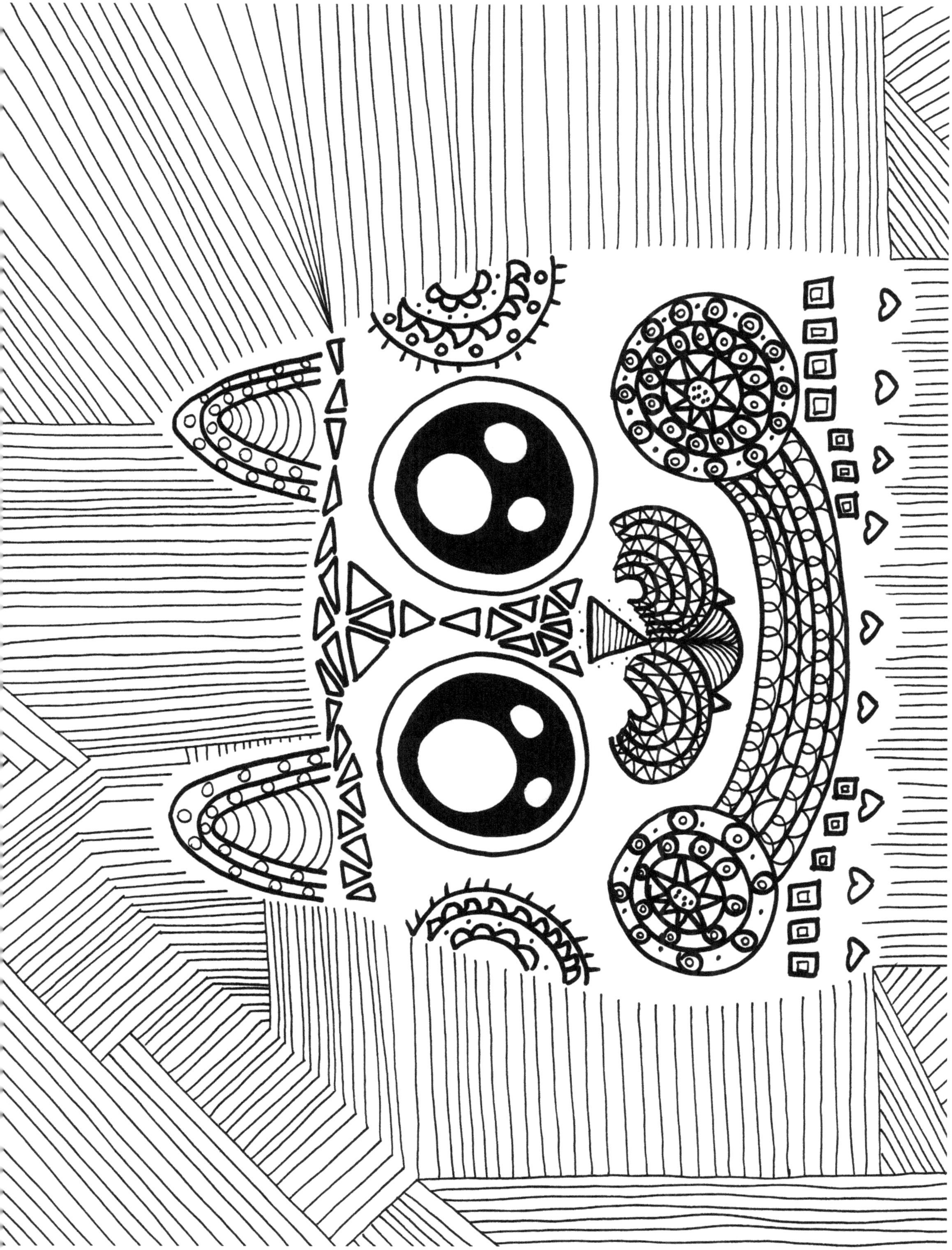

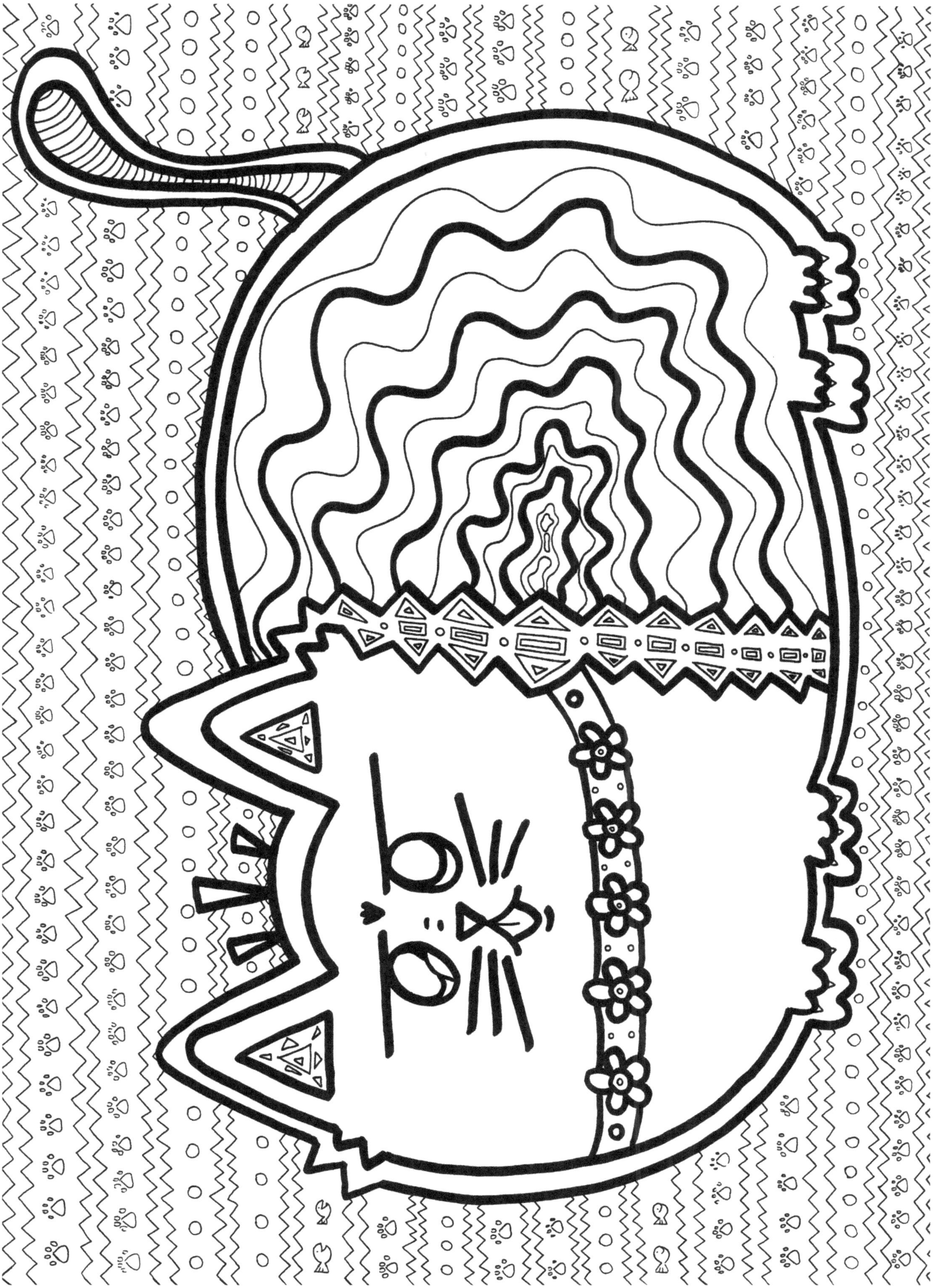

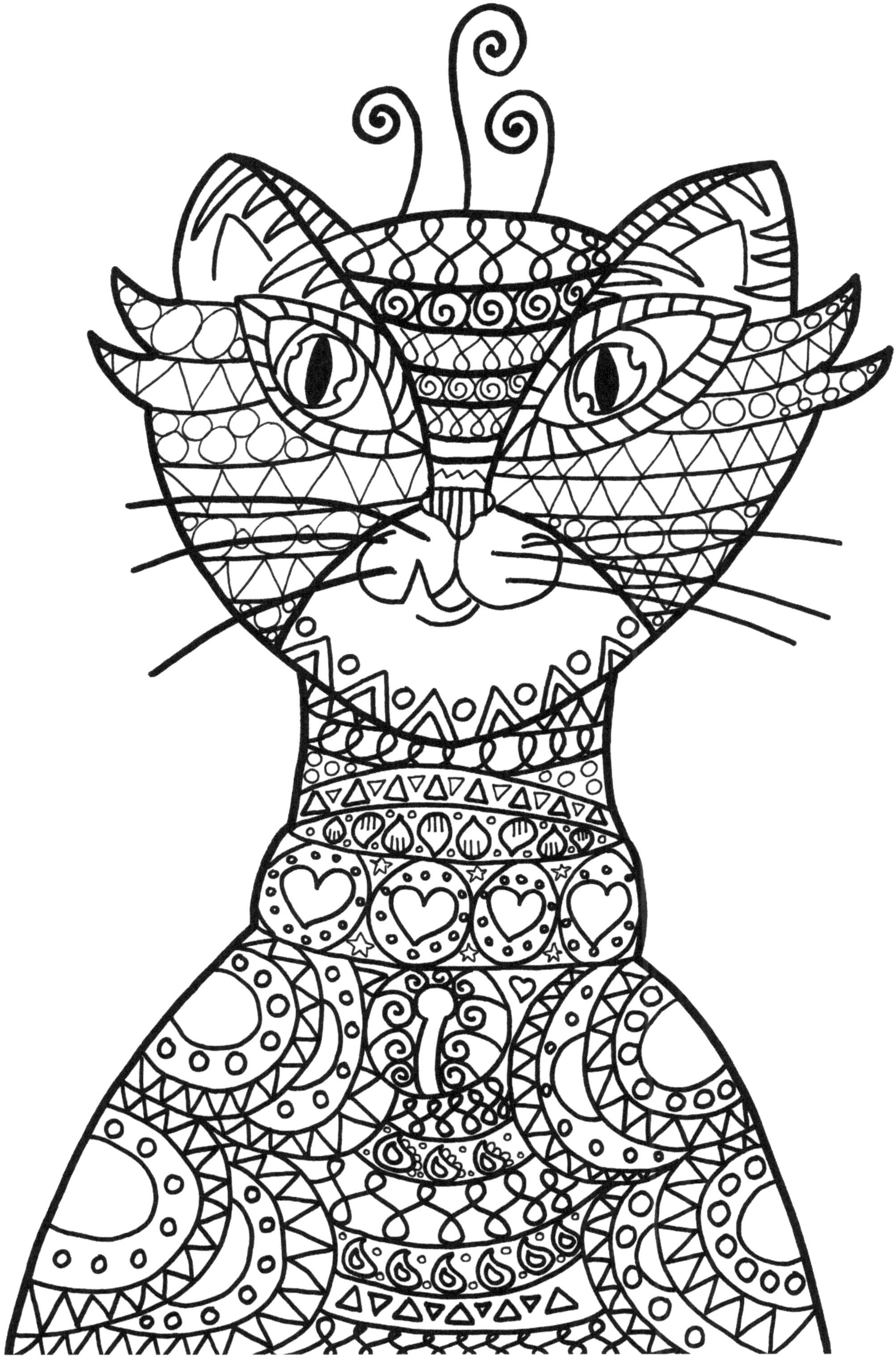

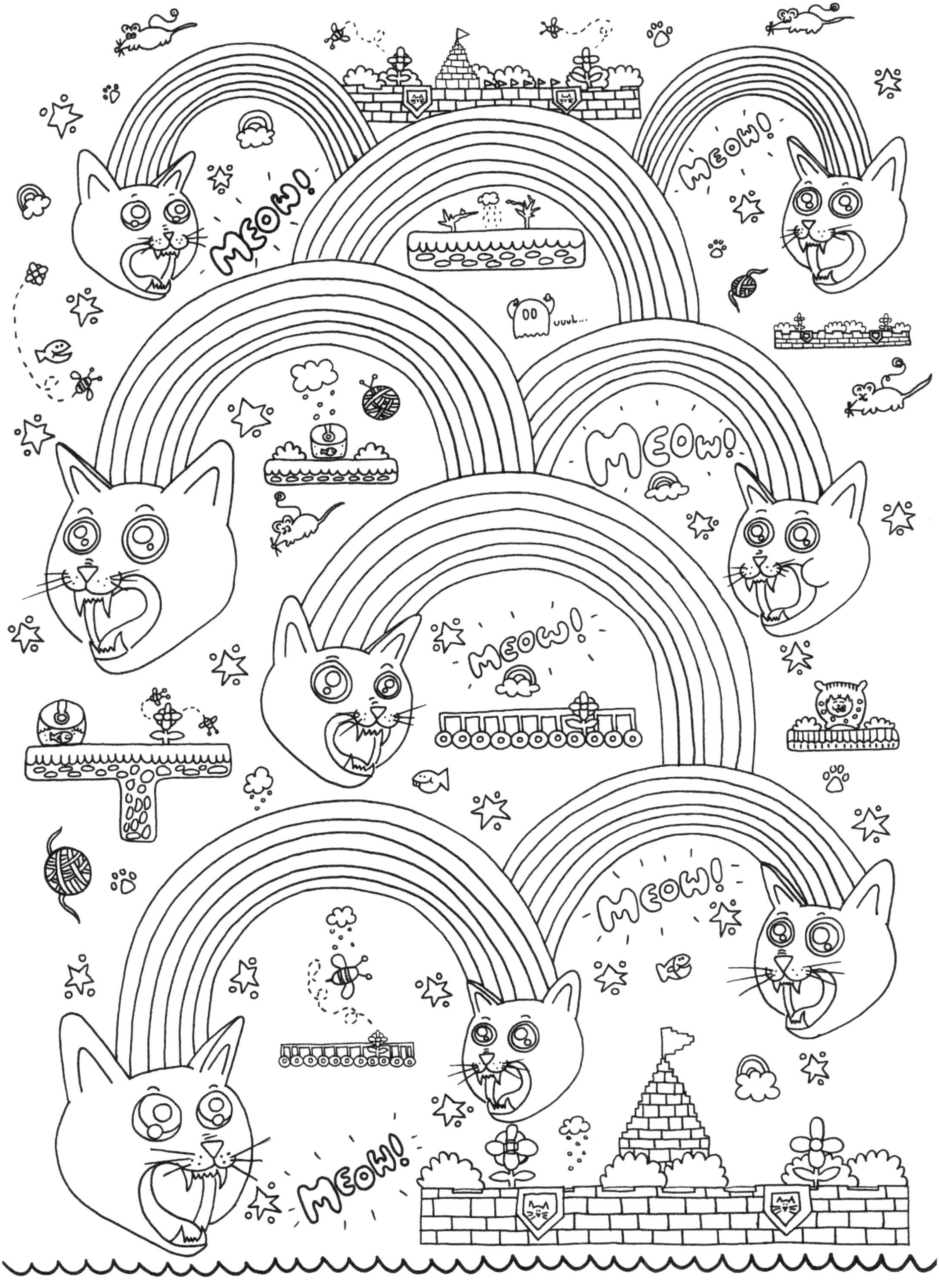
MEOW!
MEOW!
uuuh...
MEOW!
MEOW!
MEOW!
MEOW!

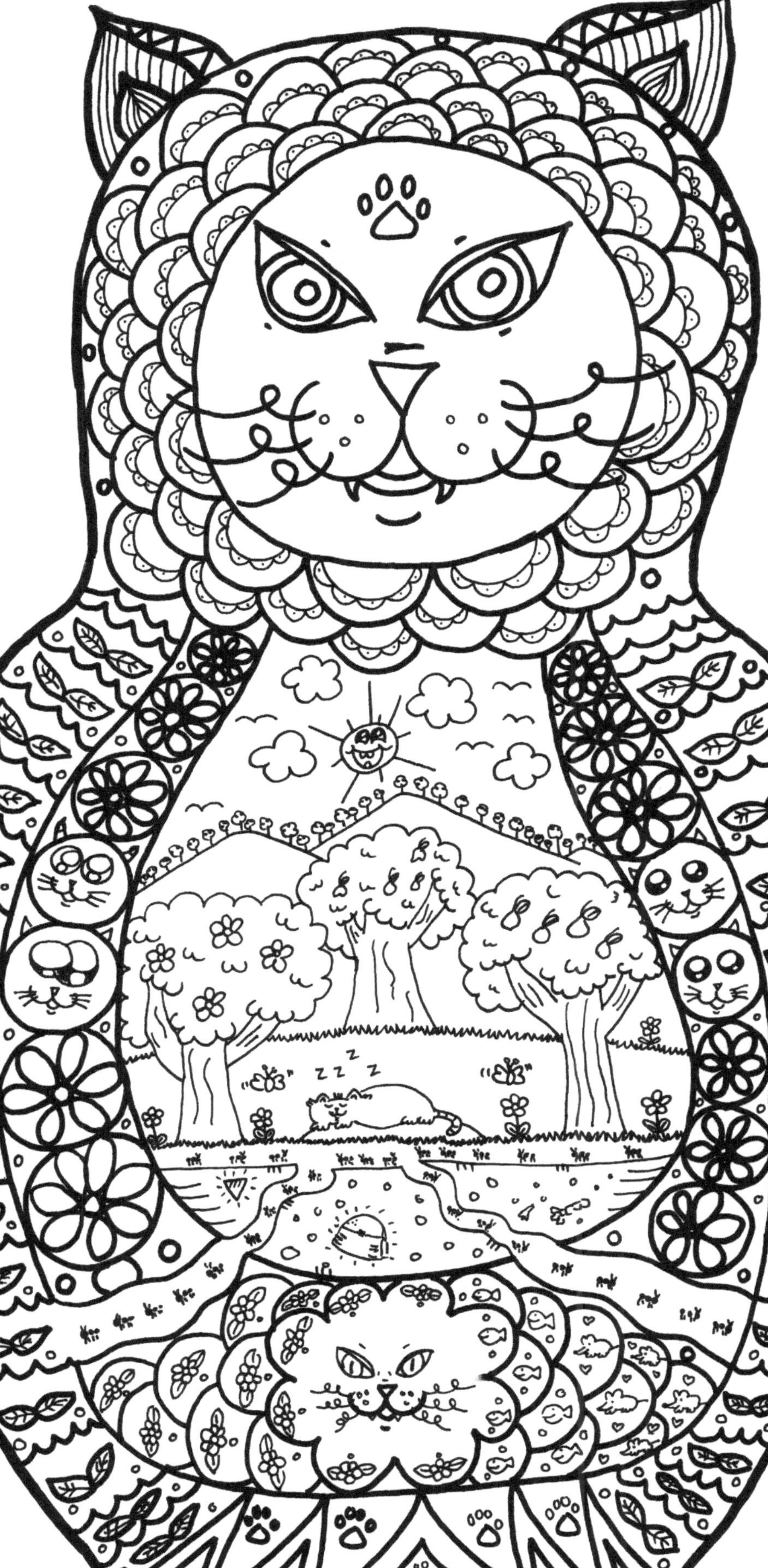

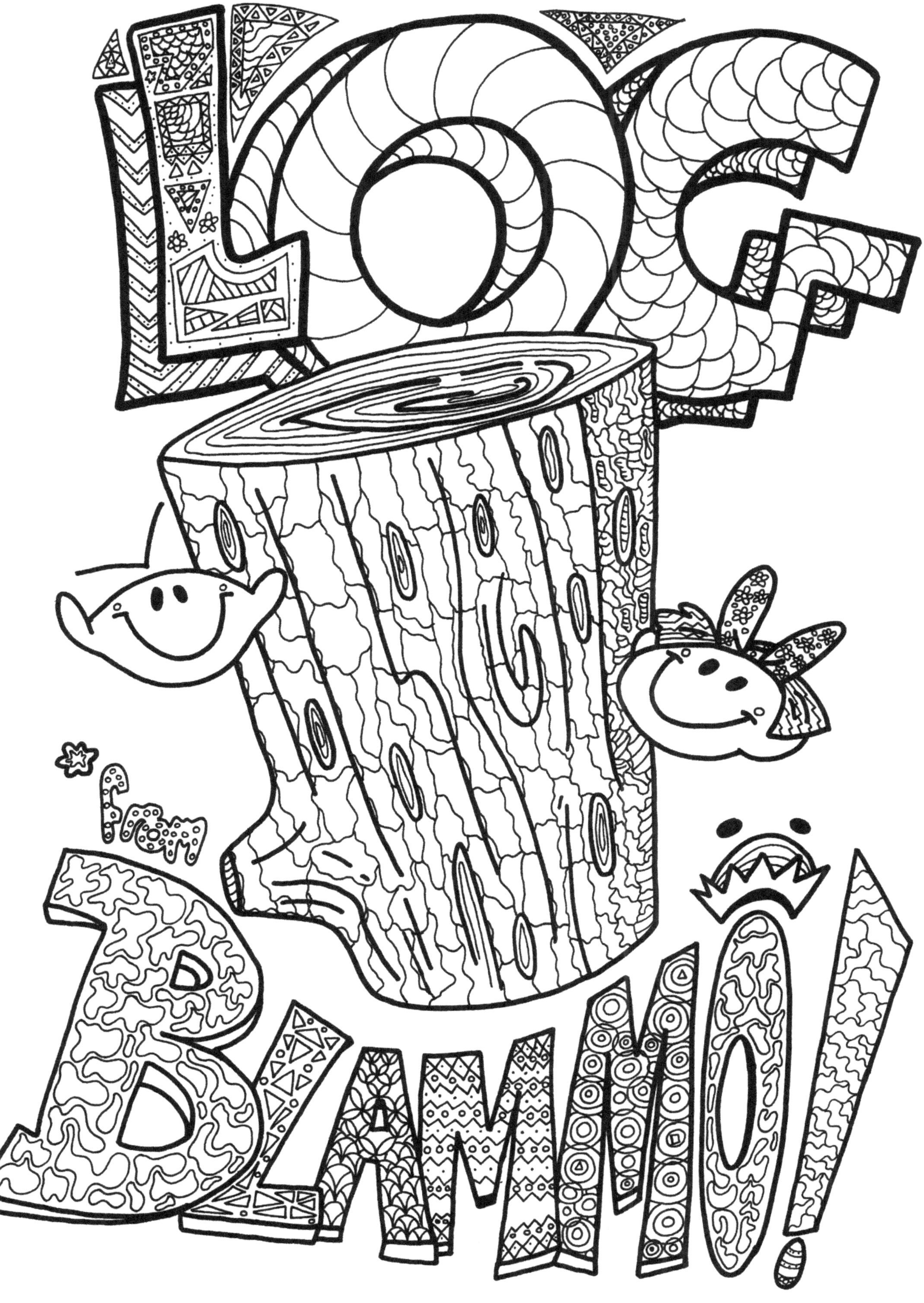
LOG
from
BLAMMO!

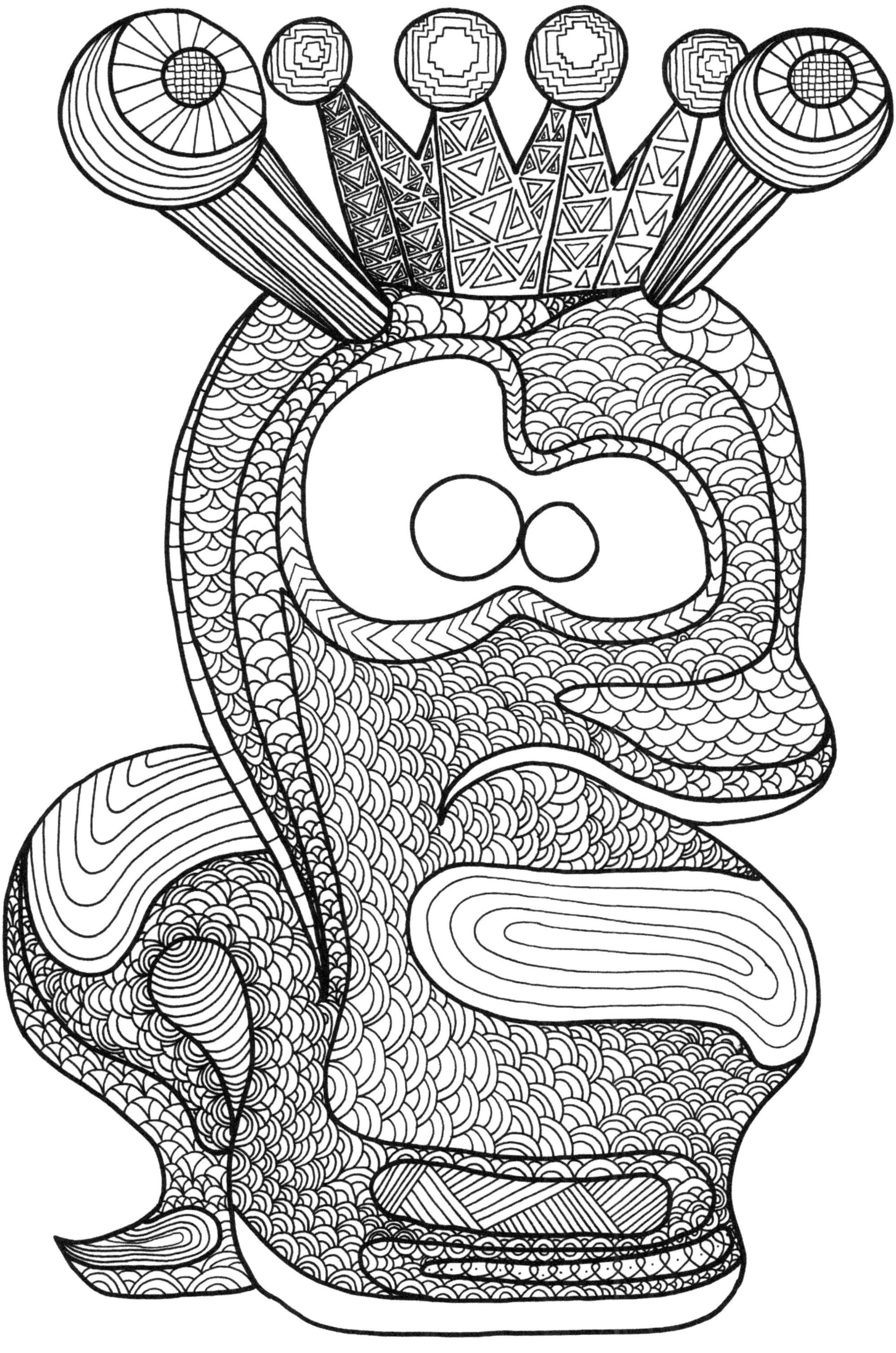

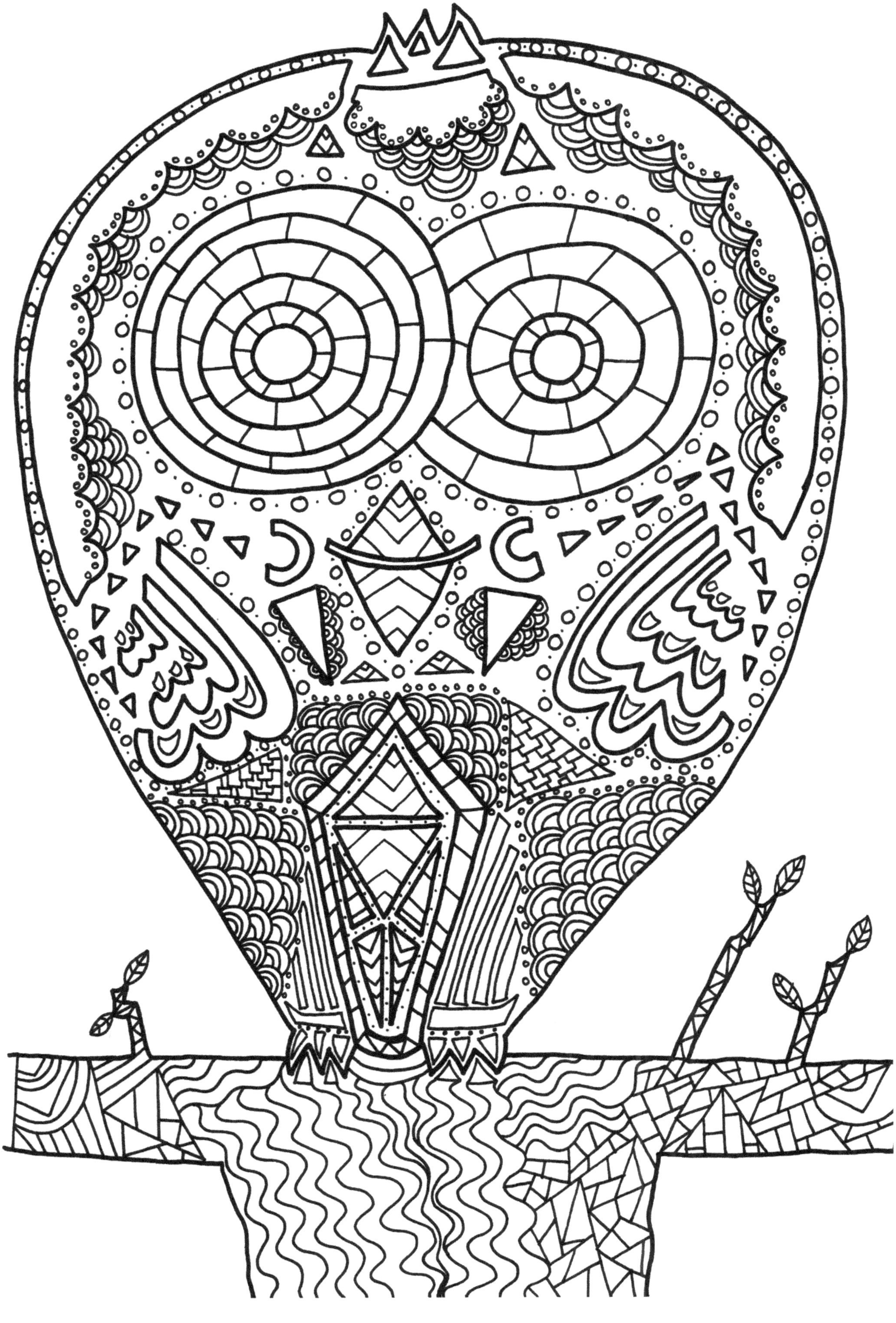

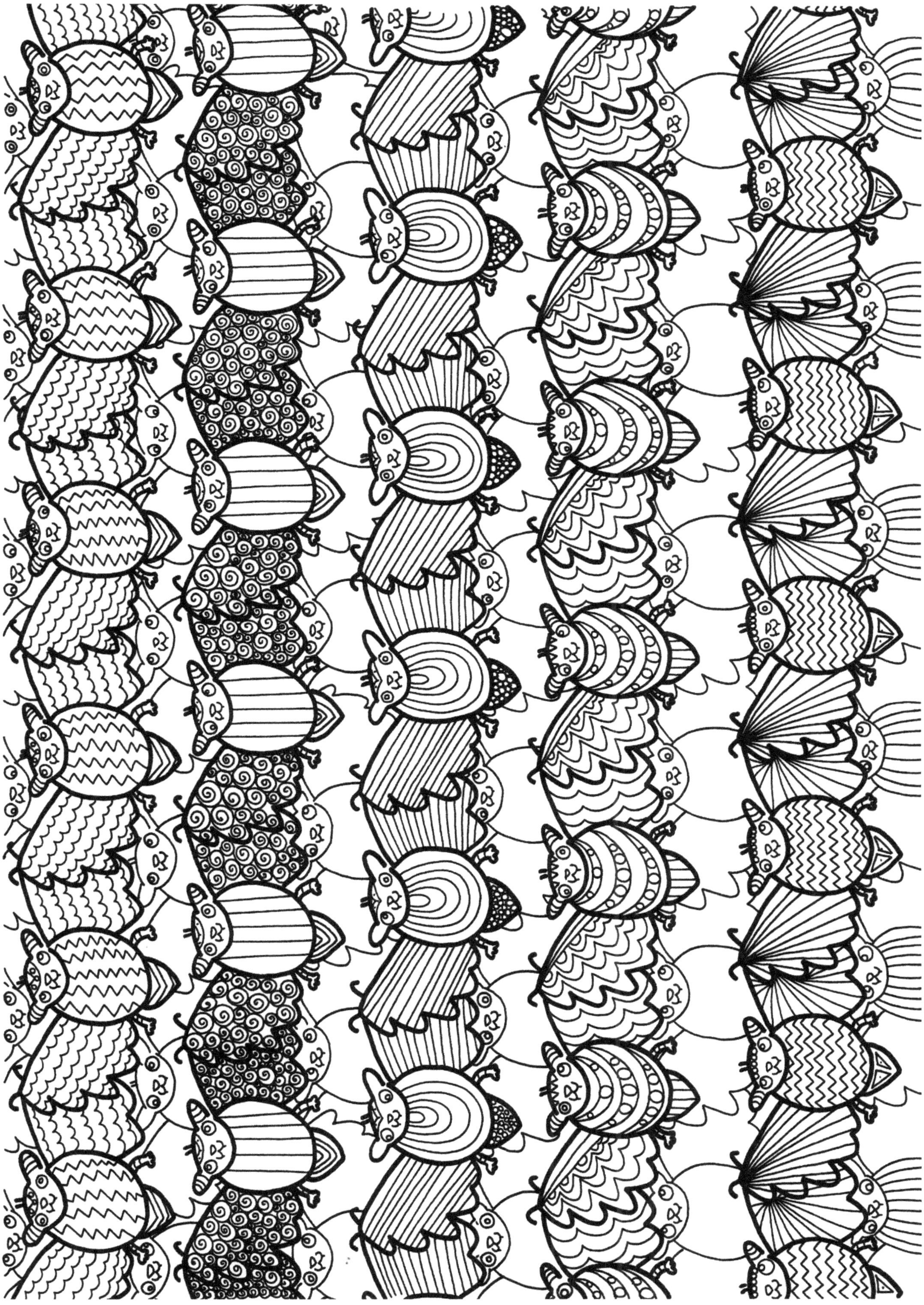

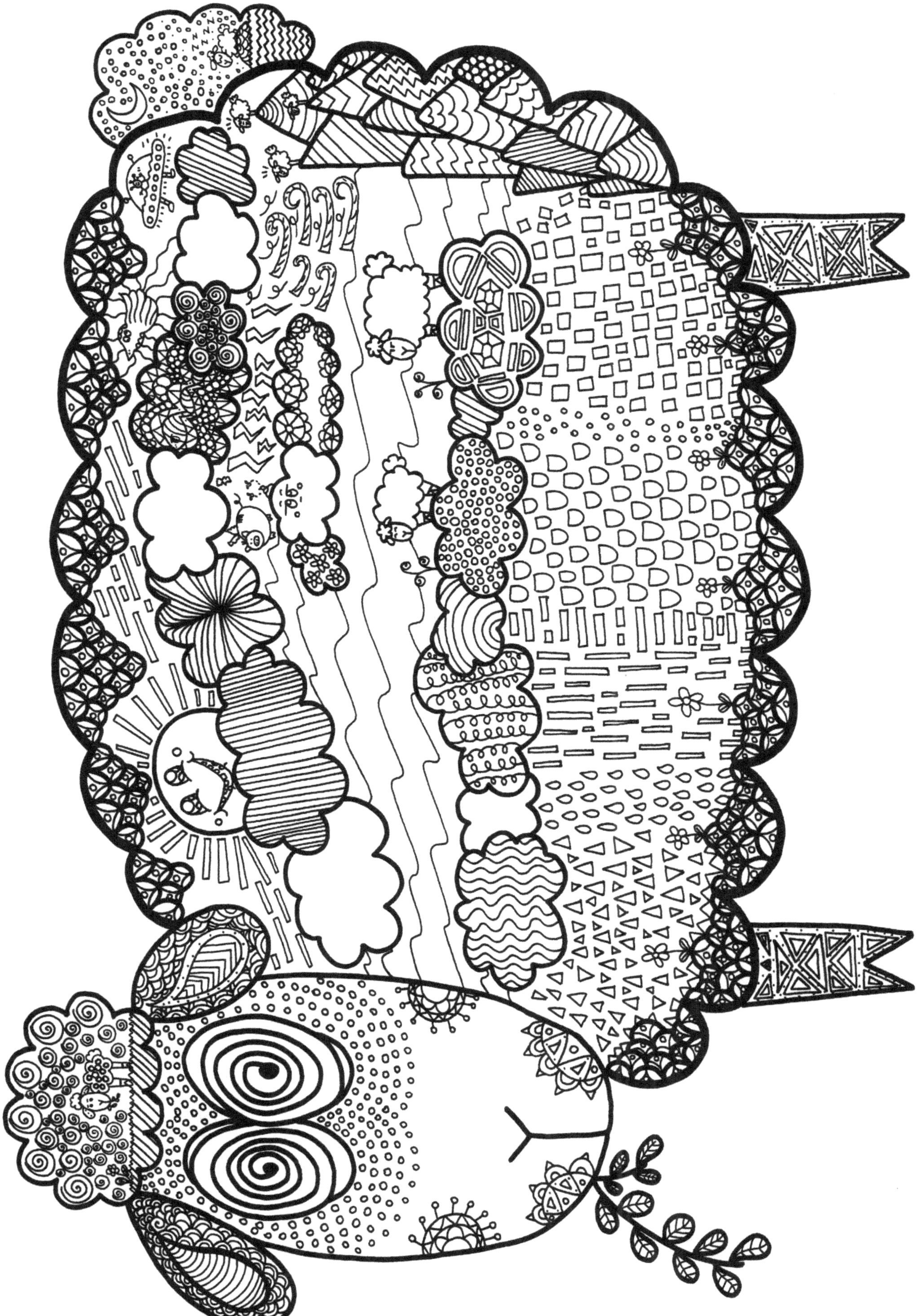

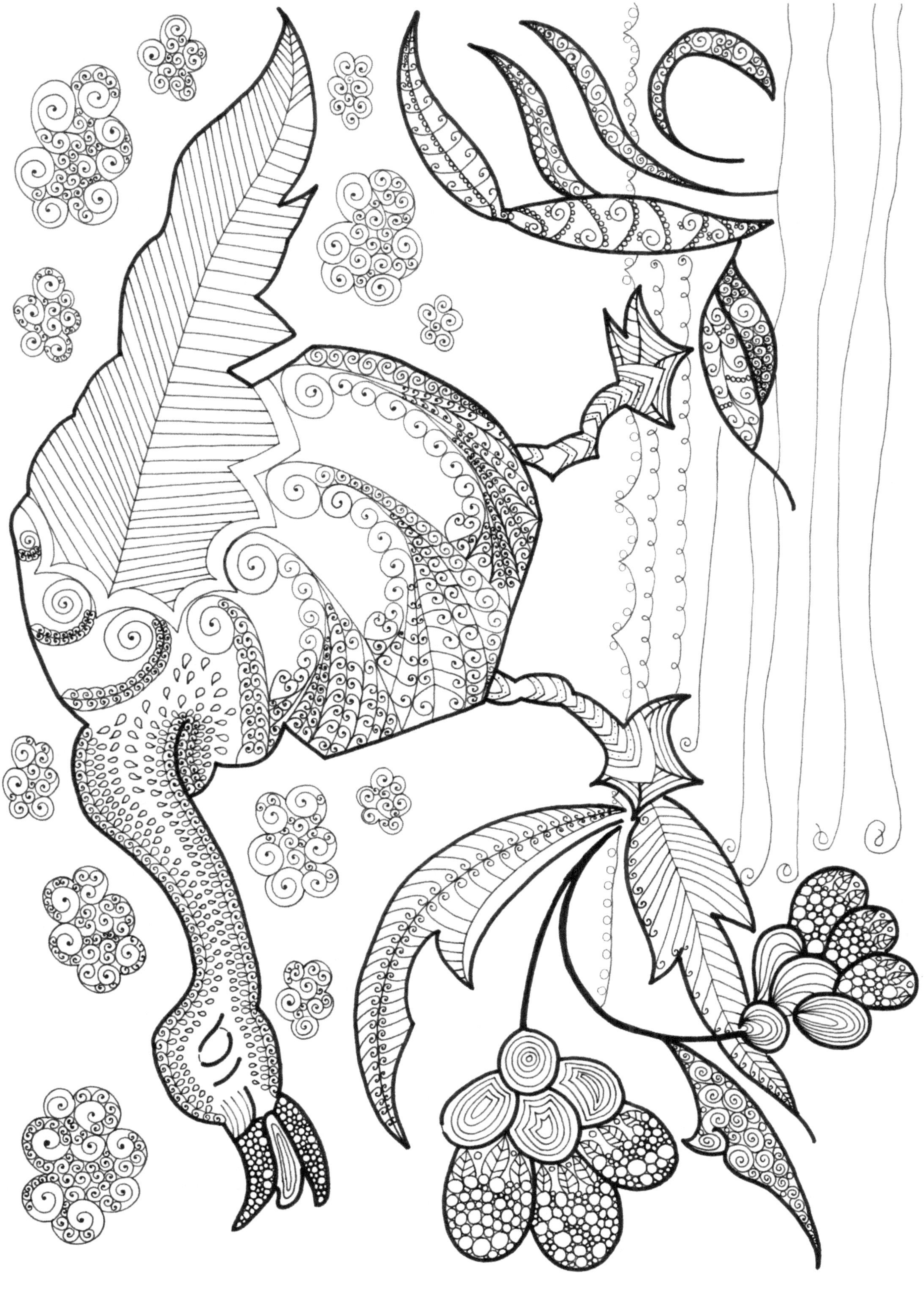

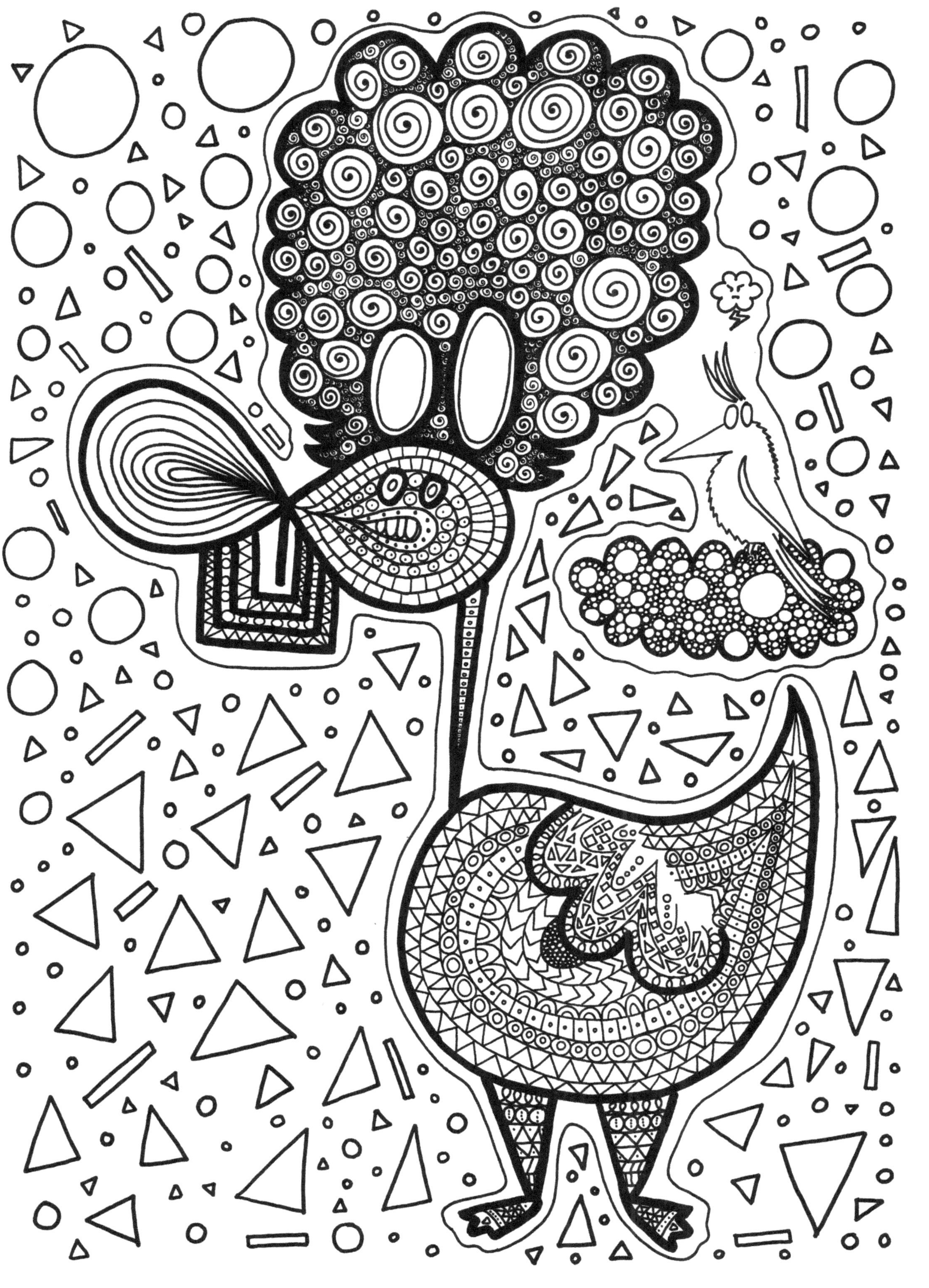

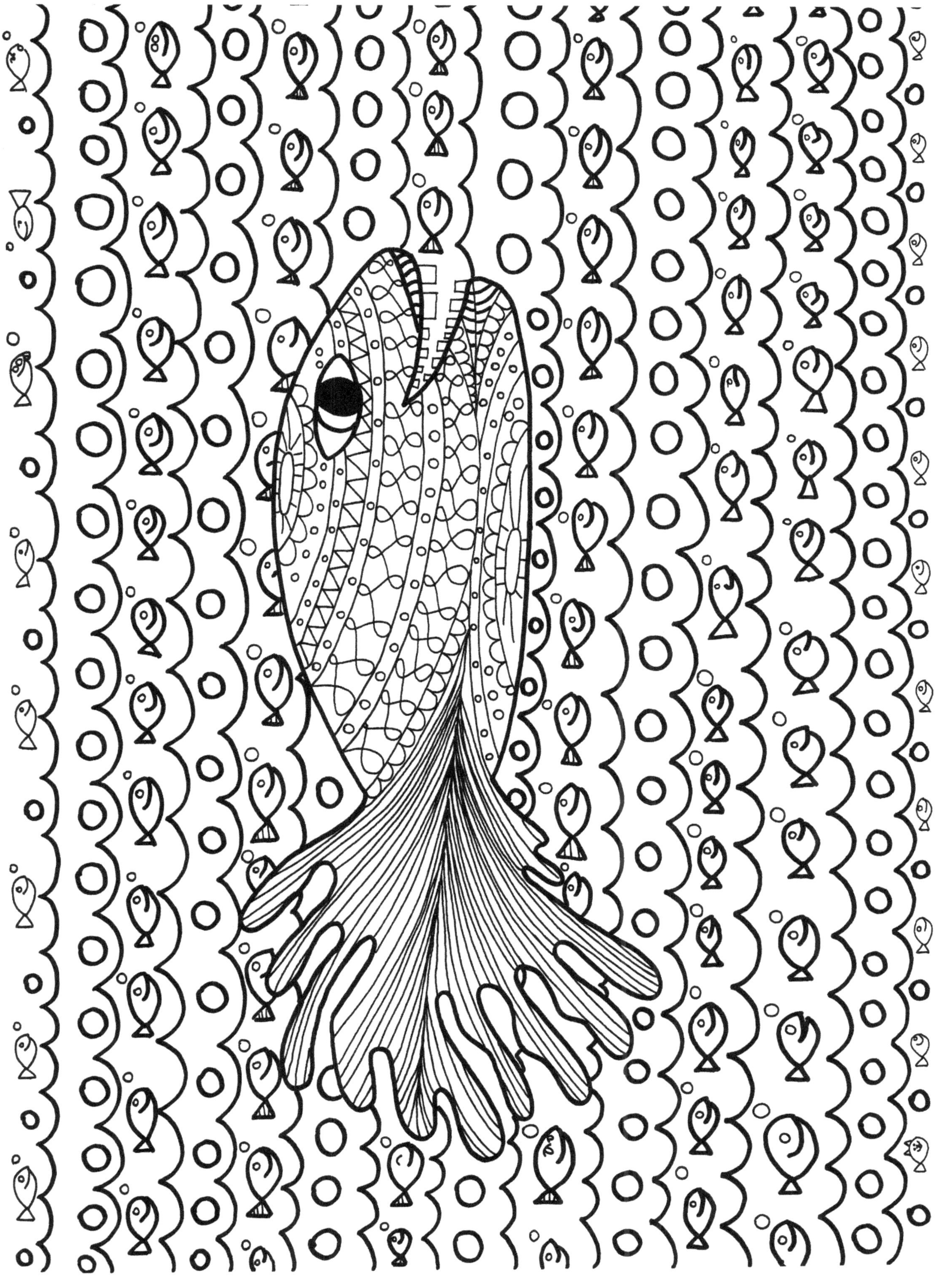

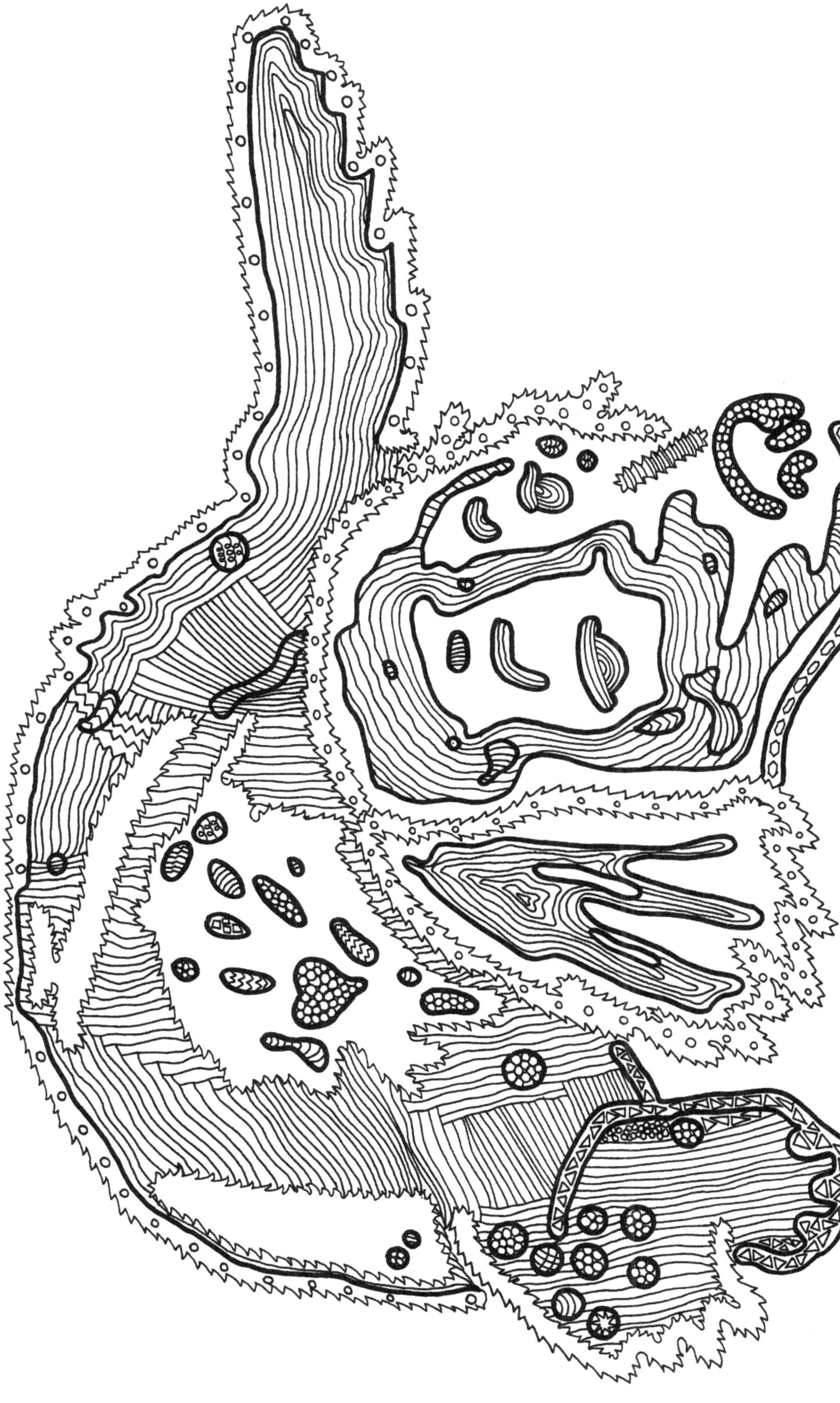

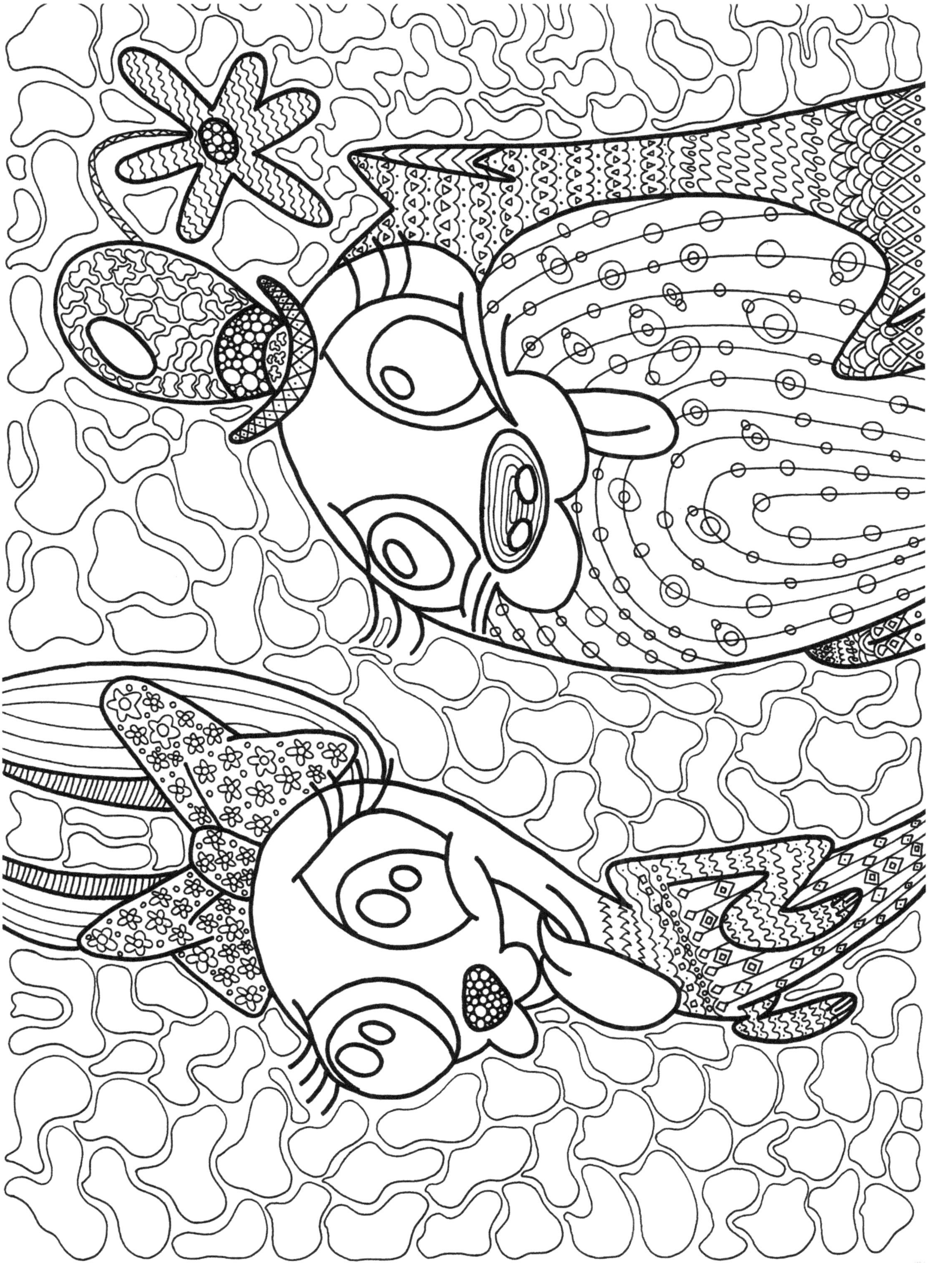

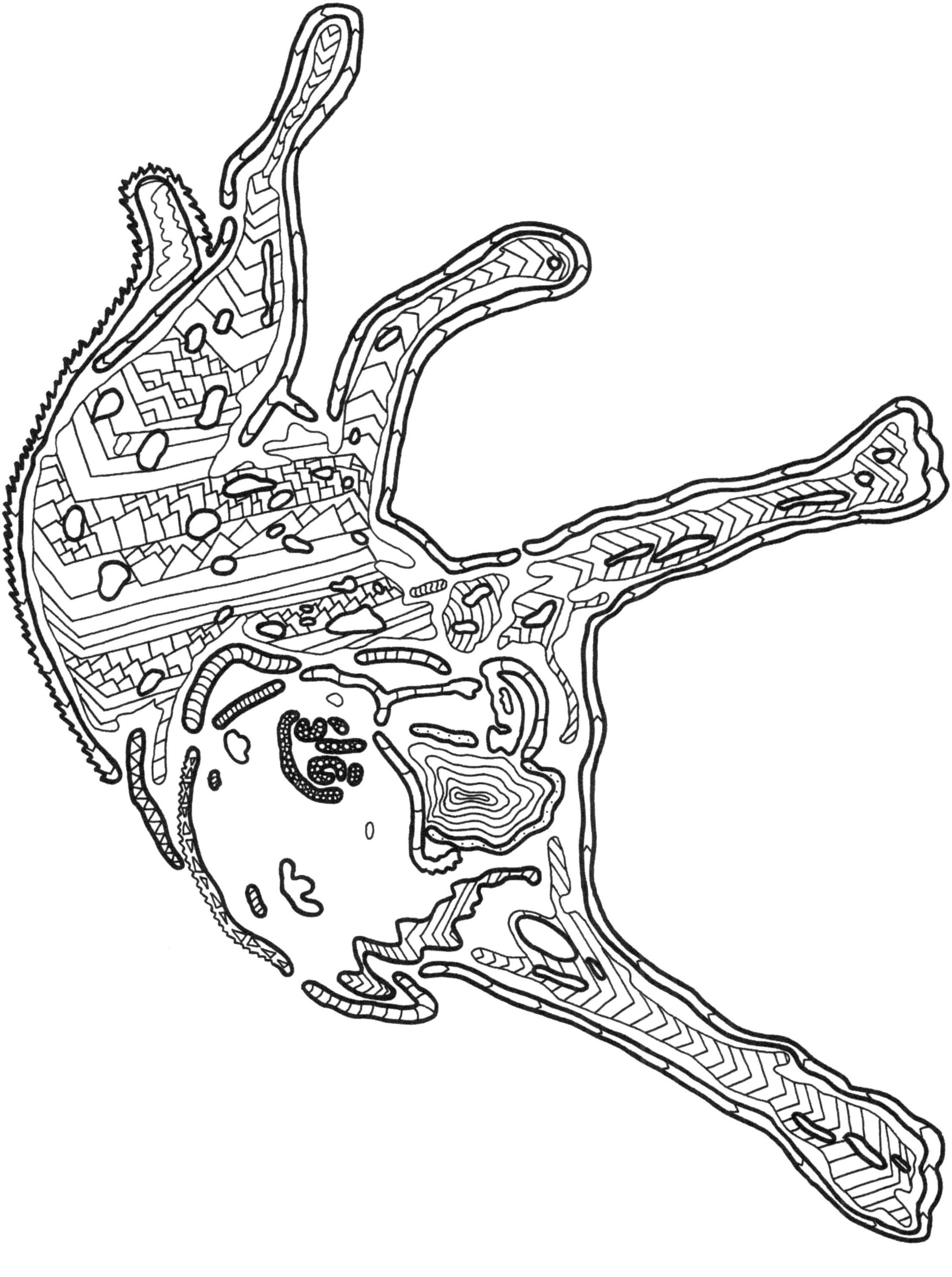

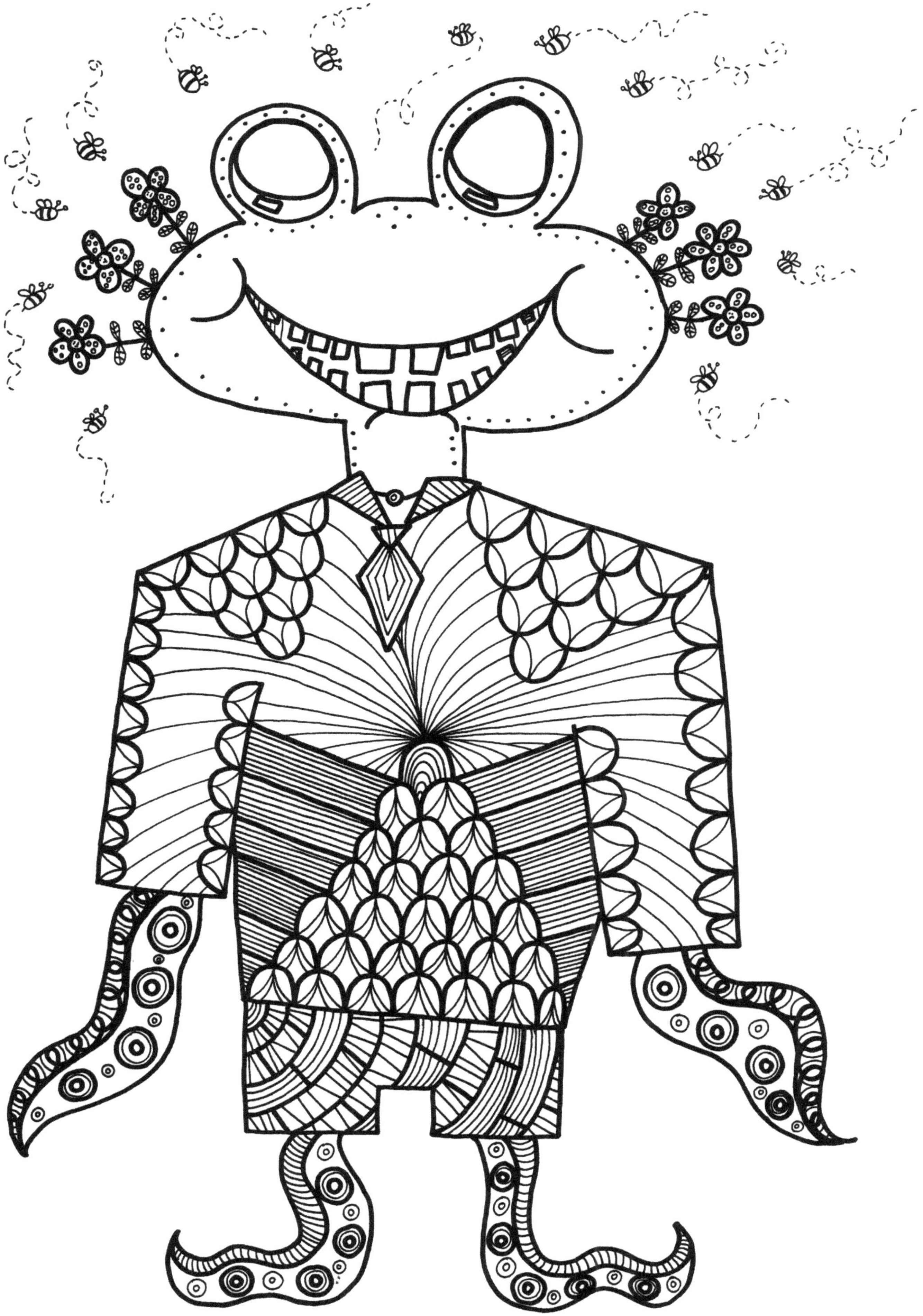

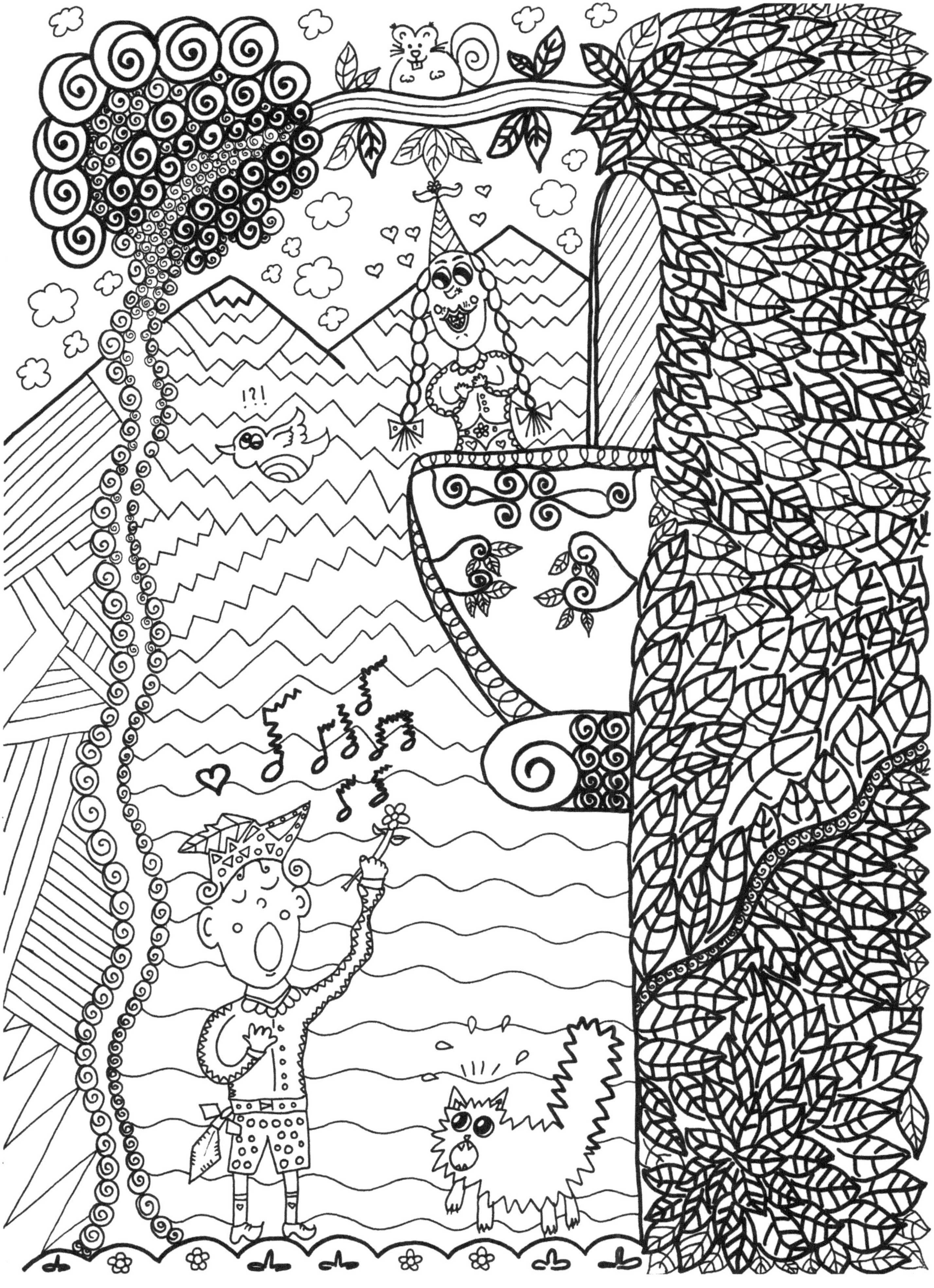

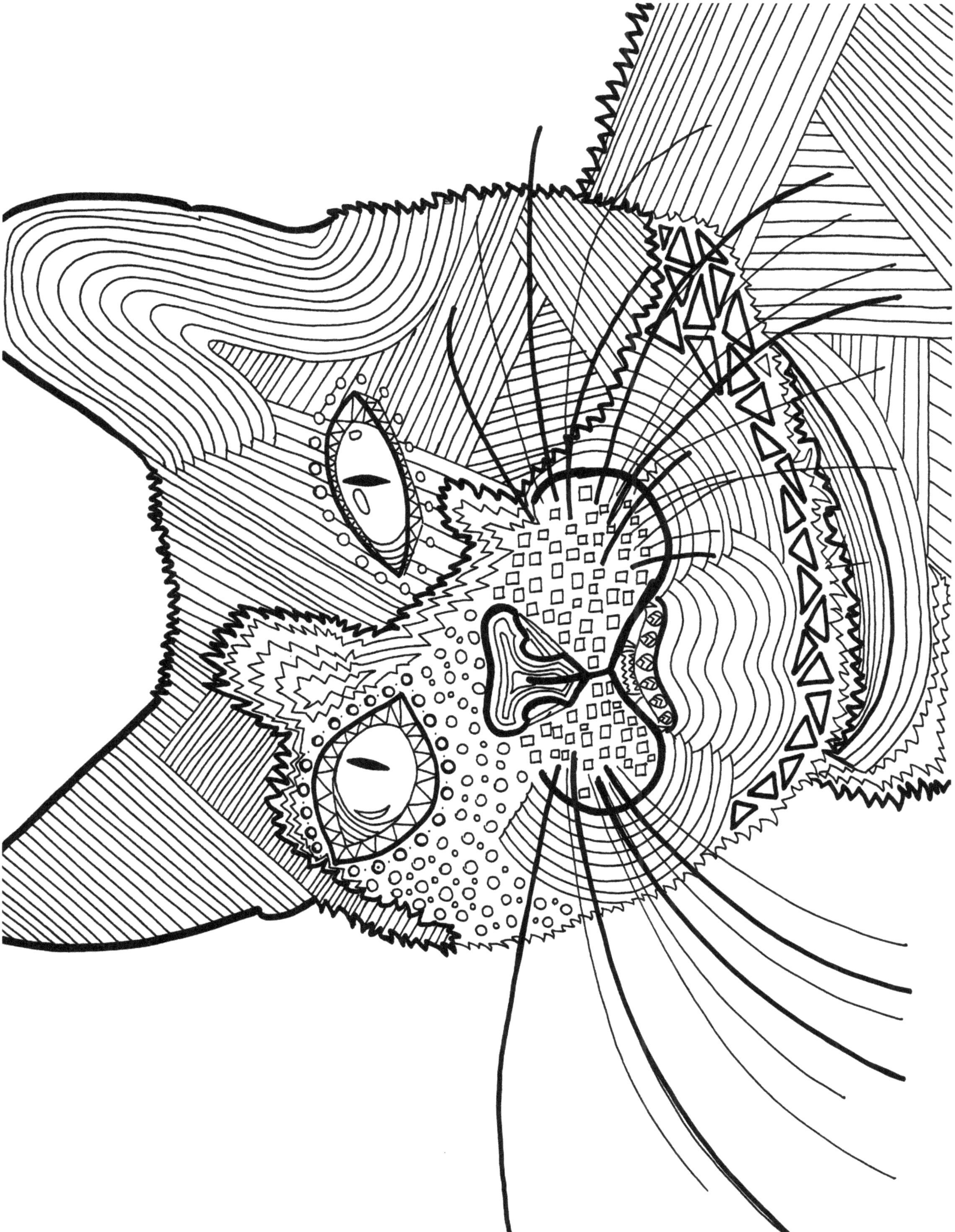

www.ingramcontent.com/pod-product-compliance
Lightning Source LLC
Chambersburg PA
CBHW081740170526
45167CB00009B/3887
* 9 7 8 1 5 4 4 0 0 8 3 9 4 *